SCHOLASTIC

ALPHA™

Grammar and Composition

2

Vaishali Batra
Series editor Anne Seaton

About ALPHA™ Grammar and Composition

Welcome to **Scholastic ALPHA™ Grammar and Composition.**

This series comprises coursebooks for classes 1 to 5 and offers an easy, engaging and meaningful way to master the skills and mechanics of English **Grammar**, **Composition** and **Comprehension**.

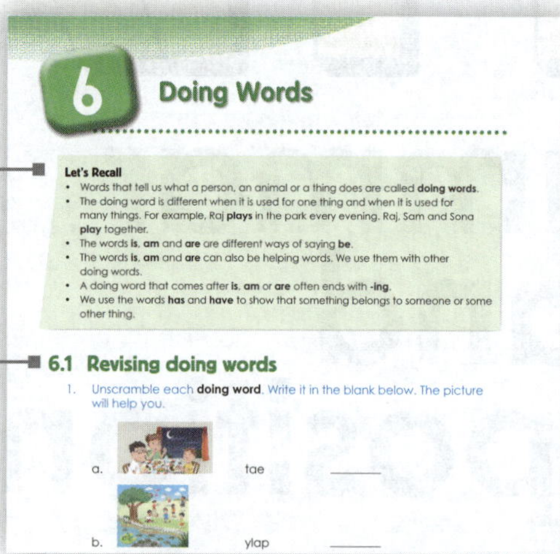
6 Doing Words

Let's Recall
- Words that tell us what a person, an animal or a thing does are called **doing words**.
- The doing word is different when it is used for one thing and when it is used for many things. For example, Raj **plays** in the park every evening. Raj, Sam and Sona **play** together.
- The words **is**, **am** and **are** are different ways of saying **be**.
- The words **is**, **am** and **are** can also be helping words. We use them with other doing words.
- A doing word that comes after **is**, **am** or **are** often ends with **-ing**.
- We use the words **has** and **have** to show that something belongs to someone or some other thing.

6.1 Revising doing words

1. Unscramble each **doing word**. Write it in the blank below. The picture will help you.

a. tae ______

b. ylap ______

Easy recall of prior topic followed by an exercise to check for readiness to learn

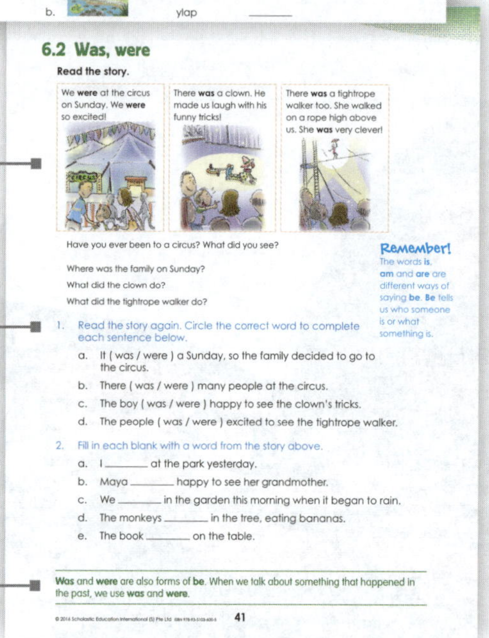
6.2 Was, were

Read the story.

We **were** at the circus on Sunday. We **were** so excited!

There **was** a clown. He made us laugh with his funny tricks!

There **was** a tightrope walker too. She walked on a rope high above us. She **was** very clever!

Have you ever been to a circus? What did you see?

Where was the family on Sunday?

What did the clown do?

What did the tightrope walker do?

Remember! The words **is**, **am** and **are** are different ways of saying **be**. **Be** tells us who someone is or what something is.

1. Read the story again. Circle the correct word to complete each sentence below.
   a. It (was / were) a Sunday, so the family decided to go to the circus.
   b. There (was / were) many people at the circus.
   c. The boy (was / were) happy to see the clown's tricks.
   d. The people (was / were) excited to see the tightrope walker.
2. Fill in each blank with a word from the story above.
   a. I ______ at the park yesterday.
   b. Maya ______ happy to see her grandmother.
   c. We ______ in the garden this morning when it began to rain.
   d. The monkeys ______ in the tree, eating bananas.
   e. The book ______ on the table.

Was and **were** are also forms of **be**. When we talk about something that happened in the past, we use **was** and **were**.

41

Grammar focus through an engaging picture story

Related exercises for meaningful learning

Simple definition to explain each grammar concept

Practice exercises for meaningful application of the concept

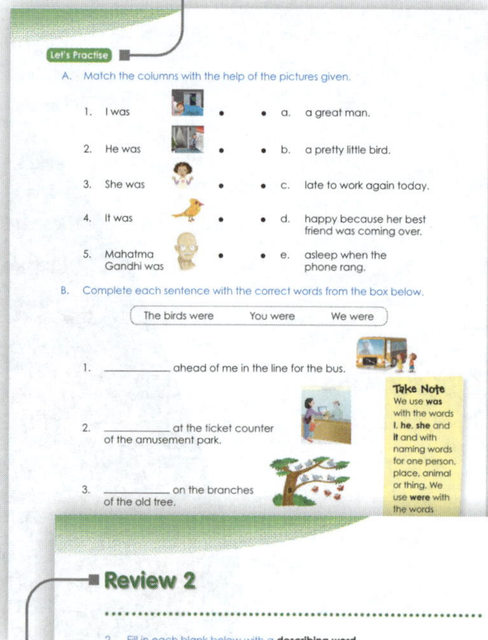
Let's Practise

A. Match the columns with the help of the pictures given.

1. I was — a. a great man.
2. He was — b. a pretty little bird.
3. She was — c. late to work again today.
4. It was — d. happy because her best friend was coming over.
5. Mahatma Gandhi was — e. asleep when the phone rang.

B. Complete each sentence with the correct words from the box below.

The birds were | You were | We were

1. ______ ahead of me in the line for the bus.
2. ______ at the ticket counter of the amusement park.
3. ______ on the branches of the old tree.

Take Note: We use **was** with the words **I**, **he**, **she** and **it** and with naming words for one person, place, animal or thing. We use **were** with the words

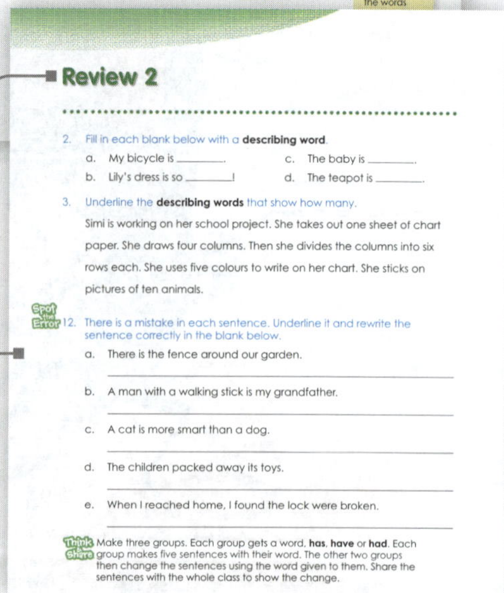
Review 2

2. Fill in each blank below with a **describing word**.
   a. My bicycle is ______.
   b. Lily's dress is so ______!
   c. The baby is ______.
   d. The teapot is ______.
3. Underline the **describing words** that show how many.

   Simi is working on her school project. She takes out one sheet of chart paper. She draws four columns. Then she divides the columns into six rows each. She uses five colours to write on her chart. She sticks on pictures of ten animals.

Spot the Error 12. There is a mistake in each sentence. Underline it and rewrite the sentence correctly in the blank below.
   a. There is the fence around our garden.
   b. A man with a walking stick is my grandfather.
   c. A cat is more smart than a dog.
   d. The children packed away its toys.
   e. When I reached home, I found the lock were broken.

Think & Share: Make three groups. Each group gets a word, **has**, **have** or **had**. Each group makes five sentences with their word. The other two groups then change the sentences using the word given to them. Share the sentences with the whole class to show the change.

Periodic reviews to consolidate learning and for systematic assessment

Spot the Error to provide an opportunity for error correction

- **Take Note** provides additional tips and exceptions to rules.
- **Think & Share** activities allow opportunity for collaborative learning.
- **Remember** enhances the understanding of the concept being taught in the unit.

 ISBN 978-93-5103-600-5

Graded exercises develop key comprehension and critical thinking skills

12 Comprehension

12.1 Similarities and differences

To understand a text better, you sometimes have to compare things in it to see how similar or different they are. This is called finding similarities and differences.

Read the description.

My Family

My name is Anu and I live in Lucknow with my parents and younger brother. My mother's name is Anita. She is tall and has short hair. She is a pilot, but she loves painting in her spare time. My father Mohit is a banker. He enjoys playing golf. He is also a great cook. My brother Udit is six years old. He goes to school with me. He loves cricket and wants to be a fast bowler. I am eight years old and I love gardening and painting. I want to be an artist when I grow up.

Take Note
A description
- often expresses the writer's feelings.
- usually uses words such as I and we.
- describes and includes details about people or places.

1. Complete the table below with information from the text.

Family member	Name	What I am	Hobby
mother			
			playing golf and cooking
me		student	
brother			

Think!
In order to find similarities and differences, you can organise the information in a table and compare each row or column.

2. Tick the correct answer for each question below. The table will help you.
   a. Which two family members enjoy painting?
      i. mother and brother ii. mother and Anu
   b. Which two family members enjoy outdoor games?
      i. father and brother ii. mother and father

76

Let's Practise

Read the table.

My friends	Favourite colour	Favourite food	Favourite sport
Sam	red	noodles	football
Tim	blue	pizza	football
Eva	pink	pasta	basketball
Ryan	blue	noodles	badminton
Tanvi	red	pasta	cricket

A. Tick the correct answer for each question below.
1. How many friends like pizza?
   a. one b. none
2. Which friends like to play football?
   a. Sam and Tim b. Eva and Ryan
3. Which friends like the colour red?
   a. Tanvi and Sam b. Eva and Tim
4. What is common between Tim and Ryan?
   a. favourite food b. favourite colour

B. Write the names of the two friends who like noodles.
_______ and _______

C. Write down one difference between Sam and Tim.
____

77

Scaffolded exercises to develop key writing skills across varied genres and topics

13 Composition

1. Look at the picture and write sentences to answer the questions below. The words in the box will help you.

park flowers jogging waving smiling bloom spring

a. What is this place?
b. What are the two girls doing?
c. What season is it? Why do you think so?
d. Write a paragraph about the picture. You may use the words in the box.

84

dry colours and water balloons	soaked in lots of different colours	all the neighbours on our street
in the park in front of my house	food and sweets	to a Holi party

B-10, South Town
New Delhi
1 March 2016

Dear Disha,

I'm writing to invite you and your family _______.
The party will be held _______
on Friday. _______ will be there
to celebrate Holi together this year. We shall have lots of
_______ to play with. There will be
yummy _______ too!
The party will begin at 10 a.m. Don't forget to come in old clothes.
They will be _______!
See you soon!
Your friend,
Ira

86

5. Look at the picture below. Write a paragraph about it.

92

Vocabulary building through engaging exercises

Word Power

Silent letters

Silent letters are letters that you can't hear when you say the word.

1. Unscramble the words with the help of the pictures given. Write them in the blanks and circle the silent letters.

a. tubmh _______ f. nkfie _______
b. twrie _______ g. bmco _______
c. neke _______ h. csalte _______
d. geridb _______ i. chtay _______
e. tghie _______ j. falc _______

Opposites

Opposites are words with completely different meanings.

1. Write each word from the box next to its opposite in the table below.

south none subtract old answer there end never different catch far late low false narrow dull

a.	add		i.	true	
b.	question		j.	wide	
c.	throw		k.	here	
d.	near		l.	same	
e.	early		m.	young	
f.	begin		n.	bright	
g.	always		o.	north	
h.	high		p.	all	

 ISBN 978-93-5103-600-5

Contents

 ISBN 978-93-5103-600-5

8 Where Words

9 Joining Words

10 Sentences

11 Punctuation

12 Comprehension

Word Power

 ISBN 978-93-5103-600-5

1 The Alphabet

Let's Recall

- The English alphabet starts with the letter **A**. It ends with the letter **Z**.
- The letters of the alphabet have a fixed order called **alphabetical order**.
- The first word of every sentence starts with a **capital letter**.
- Special names of people, places, animals and things start with a capital letter.
- Names of the days of the week start with a capital letter.
- The letters **a**, **e**, **i**, **o** and **u** are called **vowels**.

1.1 Revising the alphabet

Take Note

- When we want to know the meaning of a word, we look up a **dictionary**.
- Dictionaries follow the alphabetical order.

1. Write the words in **alphabetical order** below.

   a. ant, dog ________ c. yellow, yes, year ________

   b. jelly, ball ________ d. pasta, park, pull ________

2. Underline the words below that should begin with a **capital letter**.

   little Molly loves eating potato chips. she loves salty ones, sweet ones and even sour ones. She crunches on the big chips loudly and pops the little chips into her mouth. Little molly can eat them in the morning, afternoon and night, from sunday to saturday. She loves how crispy they are!

3. Fill in the boxes below with the names of the days of the week.

Sunday	Monday				Friday	

4. Fill in each blank below with the correct **vowel**.

a.  b.  c.  d.  e. 

__range __ggs __mbrella __eroplane __ce cream

 ISBN 978-93-5103-600-5

1.2 Capital and small letters

Read the story.

In **D**ecember every year, Tony hangs up lights around the house.

On **C**hristmas **E**ve, Celia decorates the plants in her garden.

During **C**hristmas, all the houses look pretty with their sparkling lights.

Which festival do you like best?

When does Tony hang up lights?

When does Celia decorate the plants in her garden?

When do all the houses look pretty?

1. Unscramble each special name from the story. Write the name in the blank.

   a. dcembree: D__________ b. crhistmsa: C__________

2. Look at the picture. Fill in the blanks with the help of the words in the box.

Onam	March	Guru Nanak Jayanti	Holi

My favourite festival is ________. It is usually celebrated in the month of ________. On the day of Holi we throw coloured water over each other. Bala is from Kerala. ________ is an important festival for him. Sukhbir celebrates ________, which is the birthday of Guru Nanak. My friends and I celebrate all the festivals together. We have a lot of fun!

The names of months and festivals are special names. They always start with a **capital letter**.

 ISBN 978-93-5103-600-5

Let's Practise

A. Circle the names of the twelve months of the year in the word grid below. Write them in order in the blanks.

F	E	B	R	U	A	R	Y	S
Q	M	A	Y	Z	P	L	J	E
J	A	N	U	A	R	Y	U	P
M	A	R	C	H	I	T	N	T
B	V	R	J	U	L	Y	E	E
N	O	V	E	M	B	E	R	M
Y	A	U	G	U	S	T	F	B
D	E	C	E	M	B	E	R	E
U	U	O	C	T	O	B	E	R

1. ____________ 7. ____________

2. ____________ 8. ____________

3. ____________ 9. ____________

4. ____________ 10. ____________

5. ____________ 11. ____________

6. ____________ 12. ____________

B. Look at the names of the special days in the box. Write the correct name beside each picture.

Durga Puja	Dussehra	Independence Day
Christmas	Eid	Raksha Bandhan

1.  ____________

4.  ____________

2.  ____________

5.  ____________

3.  ____________

6.  ____________

 ISBN 978-93-5103-600-5

2 Naming Words

Let's Recall

- Everything around us has a name. These names are called **naming words**.
- Names for people, places, animals and things are called **common names**.
- Some people, places, animals and things also have **special names**.
- A naming word can mean **one** or **more than one**. When we mean more than one, we usually add **-s** or **-es** to the common name.
- We add **-es** to common names ending in **-s**, **-x**, **-o**, **-ch** and **-sh** to show more than one.
- Sometimes we use a new word to show more than one.
- We use different naming words for **he** and **she**. **Grandfather**, **father**, **brother**, **boy** and **man** are **he words**. **Grandmother**, **mother**, **sister**, **girl** and **woman** are **she words**.

2.1 Revising naming words

1. Fill in the blanks below with **naming words**. The pictures will help you.

   Ravi is going to the post office today. He is sending a  ________ to his best friend in Kanpur. There are many  ________ at the post office. He joins the line. When it is his turn, he takes out some  ________ from his pocket to pay for a  ________.

2. Circle the **common names** and underline the **special names** below.
   a. Tina's parents got her a computer in June.
   b. Adam starts working at Grace Hospital soon.
   c. The children like Dr Mehra because she is good and kind.
   d. Every Wednesday, my teacher takes us out to the field to run.
   e. Ali went to the market to buy his mother some flowers.

 ISBN 978-93-5103-600-5

3. Circle the correct **words** to complete the story below.

Amit's favourite (place / places) in school is the library. He likes going there during recess to read a (book / books). His favourite books are the ones about (animal / animals). He enjoys reading about (fox / foxes) and (panda / pandas). Today he plans to relax on a (bench / benches) and read the new book about jungle animals.

4. Fill in each blank with the correct word to show **more than one**. The picture will help you.

a. two  ________ c. two  ________

b. three 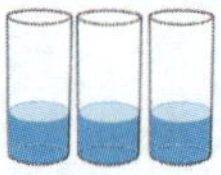 ________ d. two 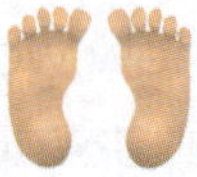 ________

5. Complete the table below with the correct **she words**. The pictures will help you.

He word		She word	
boy			
lion			
policeman			

6. Write the **he** and **she words** from the box below in the correct column.

father man sister mother woman brother

He word	She word

 ISBN 978-93-5103-600-5

2.2 One and more than one

Read the story.

Sam and Evie see some **daisies**. Evie takes a photograph of a **daisy**.

Suddenly, they walk into a swamp! "Wave your **handkerchief**!" cries Evie. Both children wave their **handkerchieves** and shout for help.

Two men run to help. Each man takes off his **scarf**. They tie the **scarves** together and pull the children out.

Look at the pictures. What do you think is a swamp?

What did Sam and Evie see? What did Evie photograph?

What did Evie tell Sam? What did they wave to get help?

What was each man wearing round his neck? What did they tie together?

Take Note
To show more than one handkerchief we can write **handkerchiefs** or **handkerchieves**.

1. Read the story again. Then match the columns below.

a.	scarf	i.	daisies
b.	handkerchief	ii.	scarves
c.	daisy	iii.	handkerchieves

2. Match each picture with the naming word below.

a. 

b. 

c. 

d. 

i. knife   ii. monkey   iii. butterflies   iv. leaves

For naming words that end in **-y**, we replace the **-y** with **-ies** to show **more than one**.
We replace the **-f** and **-fe** endings of naming words with **-ves** to show more than one.

Think & Share Pair up with a classmate. List as many naming words as you can that end in **-y**, **-f** and **-fe** in a column. Write the naming word to show more than one in the next column. Compare your list with your partner's.

 ISBN 978-93-5103-600-5

Let's Practise

A. Fill in each blank with the help of the picture given. Change **-y** to **-ies** for naming words that show **more than one**.

1. five  ________
2. one  ________
3. one  ________
4. many  ________
5. three  ________
6. two  ________

B. Fill in each blank with the help of the word given in the brackets. Change **-f** or **-fe** to **-ves** for naming words that show **more than one**.

1. There are two ________ of bread on the shelf. (loaf)
2. Children should stay away from ________. (knife)
3. I saw a ________ in the jungle. (wolf)
4. The books are on the last ________. (bookshelf)
5. Snow White lived in a cottage with seven ________. (dwarf)
6. Two ________ broke into Mr Verma's house last night. (thief)

C. Circle the correct spelling of each naming word that shows **more than one**.

1.	half	halfs / halves
2.	shelf	shelfs / shelves
3.	monkey	monkeys / monkies
4.	body	bodys / bodies
5.	city	citys / cities
6.	toy	toys / toyes
7.	story	storys / stories
8.	leaf	leafs / leaves
9.	tray	trays / trayes
10.	spy	spys / spies

Take Note
When we show more than one for a naming word that ends in **a vowel and y**, we just add **-s** to it, e.g. **key** + **s** = **keys**.

 ISBN 978-93-5103-600-5

2.3 He and she

Read the story.

"May I feed the **cows**?" Kim asks her **aunt**.

"Look out!" shouts their **uncle** from the gate.

"Run!" yells their **aunt**. "There's a **bull** behind us!"

What do you think happens next?

What does Kim want to feed?

Who shouts from the gate?

What was chasing them?

1. Fill in each blank with a word from the story above.

a. a woman: ________ c. a she animal: ________

b. a man: ________ d. a he animal: ________

2. Write the naming words from the box below in the correct crown.

duke	empress	emperor	lord	duchess	lady

He

____

____

____

She

____

____

____

We use different naming words to show if a person or an animal is a **he** or a **she**.

 ISBN 978-93-5103-600-5

Let's Practise

A. Fill in each blank with the correct **he** or **she word** from the box below. The picture will help you.

cows	rams	hen	niece

1. The ________  lays eggs, but the cock does not.
2. There are so many sheep here! Can you tell which ones are ewes and which are ________ ?
3. Every morning, little Jack helps Farmer Yazir milk the ________ .
4. Mrs Mirza invited her nephew and ________  to her new house.

B. Complete the table below with **he** and **she words**.

He words	She words
drake	
	goddess
waiter	
	cow
bridegroom	
	vixen
sir	
	granddaughter

C. Fill in each blank below with the correct word from the brackets.

1. Mr Rahman is my ____________ (landlord/landlady).
2. My mum's brother is my ____________ (aunt/uncle).
3. My cousin Sunaina is my mum's ____________ (nephew/niece).
4. My cousin Shiv is my mum's ____________ (nephew/niece).
5. Shah Jahan was a Mughal ____________ (emperor/empress).
6. Mumtaz Mahal was Shah Jahan's ____________ (emperor/empress).

 ISBN 978-93-5103-600-5

2.4 Words that show belonging

Read the story.

Mrs Brown**'s** house is full of photos. She likes to look at her family**'s** photos every day.

Her son David**'s** family visits her every summer. The children love listening to their grandmother**'s** stories.

David**'s** children enjoy looking at old albums. "That's Grandfather**'s** photo," he tells them.

Who else do you think will be in the album?

Whose house has old photos?

What do the children love doing?

Whose photo do the children see in the album?

1. Fill in each blank with a word from the story above.

   a. ____________ album has many photos of her son.

   b. I go to my ____________ house during the school holidays.

   c. ____________ mother loves her grandchildren.

2. Circle each naming word below that shows something belongs to it.

   a. Sam's spectacles are red. 

   b. Anita's ball is orange. 

   c. Abdul is holding his mother's hand. 

   d. My sister's books are tied up in bundles. 

We add an **'s** to a naming word to show that something belongs to it.

 ISBN 978-93-5103-600-5

Let's Practise

A. Fill in each blank by adding **'s** to the naming word given in the brackets to show belonging. The picture will help you.

1. __________ (Amy) toys are on the floor. 

2. The __________ (cat) teeth are sharp. 

3. Sam likes __________ (Dean) shoes. 

4. The __________ (giraffe) neck is very long. 

5. The children are playing in __________ (Jenny) pool. 

6. Rita likes __________ (Seema) book collection. 

B. Tick the correct word to complete each sentence below.

1. My ____ old coat is too big for me.

   a. brothers b. brothers' c. brother's

2. Radha found ____ notebook.

   a. Alishas b. Alisha's c. Alishas'

3. Jessica put on her ____ raincoat.

   a. sisters b. sisters' c. sister's

4. The dog found ____ ball.

   a. Sumit's b. Sumits' c. Sumits

5. The book was under ____ computer.

   a. Mum's b. Mums' c. Mums

 ISBN 978-93-5103-600-5

3 Other Naming Words

Let's Recall

- The words **I**, **we**, **you**, **he**, **she**, **it**, **they**, **this**, **that**, **these** and **those** can take the place of naming words.
- **I**, **you**, **he**, **she** and **it** are used to show that there is one of the naming word.
- **We**, **you** and **they** are used to show that there are more than one of the naming word.
- We use **this** for a naming word near us. We use **that** for a naming word far from us.
- We use **these** for naming words near us. We use **those** for naming words far from us.

3.1 Revising other naming words

1. The underlined words used in place of the naming words are incorrect. Rewrite the sentences using the correct words. The pictures will help you.

a. My name is Dr Joshi. She am a doctor. 

____

b. Here is my assistant, Sonali. It helps me attend to my patients.

____

c. Sonali and I work together. She take care of the sick.

____

d. The hospital is a busy place. He gets many patients every day.

____

e. This is Raman. We is studying to become a doctor too.

____

 ISBN 978-93-5103-600-5

2. Fill in each blank with the correct word from the box below. You may use some words more than once.

this	that	these	those

a. I like the pretty bowls on the top shelf. What is the price of ________?

b. ________ look like muddy footprints. I wonder how they got here.

c. Who is ________ ringing the bell?

d. ________ is a great place to learn skating. I come here every day.

e. Look over there! ________ look like rain clouds.

f. Those bananas look raw but ________ look ripe.

3. Write five sentences about the picture below. Include the words **this**, **that**, **these** and **those** in your sentences.

____

____

____

____

____

____

____

____

 ISBN 978-93-5103-600-5

3.2 Me, us, you, him, her, it, them

Read the story.

David asked Amy to go with **him** to a concert given by his favourite bands.

Amy got lost and asked people to help **her** find the theatre.

At last she found **it**! The bands were getting ready to play. She was glad she hadn't missed **them**!

Who was waiting for Amy at the theatre?

What did David ask Amy?

What did Amy do when she got lost?

Why was Amy glad?

1. From the story above, match each naming word with the word used in its place.

a.	David	i.	her
b.	Amy	ii.	them
c.	theatre	iii.	him
d.	bands	iv.	it

2. Fill in each blank with the help of the picture given.

a. The strong wind blew two of the balloons away. The man ran after ________.

b. We are very happy. The musician is going to play for ________.

c. "I am so excited! My parents are taking ________ to the aquarium today," said Lisa.

d. "I am going to teach ________ naming words today," said Mrs Mishra.

We use **me**, **us**, **you**, **him**, **her**, **it** and **them** in place of naming words.

 ISBN 978-93-5103-600-5

Let's Practise

A. Circle the correct word to complete each sentence below.

1. Robin was walking home when an apple suddenly fell on (he / him).
2. My cousins were waiting for (I / me) at the bus station.
3. Our dog tries to run away whenever we want to give (it / you) a bath.
4. Last Tuesday was a special day for all of (me / us).

Take Note
We use **me**, **him**, **her** and **it** in place of naming words that show one. We use **us** and **them** in place of naming words that show more than one. **You** is used for both one and more than one.

B. Fill in each blank below with **me**, **you**, **him**, **her** or **it**. The picture will help you.

1. "Look at ________! I am on the swing," cried Meg.

2. Jerry kicked the ball very hard and ________ went right into the net.

3. When Dad came home, Zaheer ran to greet ________.

4. "Bye, Lenny!" said Mum. "I shall pick ______ up after school."

C. Look at each underlined word below. Fill in the blank with the naming word or words it talks about.

1. My best friend is Mita. I like playing with <u>her</u>. ____________
2. Today, Helda brought her pet dog out to play. She gave <u>it</u> a bone to chew on. ____________
3. Tina and her brother had a fight and she hit <u>him</u> on the nose! ____________
4. "You can trust <u>me</u> with your secret," said Jean. ____________

Think & Share Write five sentences using the words **me**, **us**, **you**, **him**, **her** or **them** about the person sitting next to you. Read out the sentences in class.

 ISBN 978-93-5103-600-5

Review 1

1. Read the text below. Underline the words that should begin with a **capital letter**.

   spring is my favourite season of the year. spring comes after winter. it begins in february and continues till april. in spring, the days get longer and warmer. new leaves grow on trees and beautiful flowers bloom everywhere in spring. my favourite festival also comes in spring. it is holi, the festival of colours. people celebrate holi in february or march.

2. Make a drawing of your favourite festival in the box given. Then write five sentences about it in the blanks below.

____

____

____

____

____

____

____

 ISBN 978-93-5103-600-5

3. Find the names of six months of the year in the jumble of letters below. Write them in the blanks.

AMAYHYTSDAUGUSTNCKLJANUARYHOALOCTOBERVCPOMARCHBCAPRILTM

a. ______________________ d. ______________________

b. ______________________ e. ______________________

c. ______________________ f. ______________________

4. Change the words below from one to **more than one**.

a. child ____________ f. family ____________

b. key ____________ g. elf ____________

c. person ____________ h. day ____________

d. hoof ____________ i. life ____________

e. wife ____________ j. enemy ____________

5. Look at each **he word** given in the brackets. Fill in the blank with the correct **she word**.

a. A ____________ trotted along the path by my house. (bull)

b. My ____________ lives in Singapore. (uncle)

c. The ____________ sat on the grand throne. (emperor)

d. Mr Sinha's ____________ is a dentist. (nephew)

e. The ____________ plays with the cubs in the den. (tiger)

f. Mr Wright's ____________ is a singer. (son)

g. A famous ____________ visited our school today. (actor)

h. The evil ____________ put a curse on Sleeping Beauty. (wizard)

6. Make a sentence with each **he word** below. The pictures will help you.

a. fireman: ____ 

b. man: ____ 

c. fox: ____ 

d. drake: ____ 

e. waiter: ____ 

 ISBN 978-93-5103-600-5

7. Add **'s** to each naming word below to show belonging. Then make a sentence with it. The words in the box will help you.

claws	handle	sister	books	car	captain	window

Example The cat's claws are very sharp.

a. The teacher ________________________________.

b. Nita ________________________________.

c. This knife ________________________________.

d. My uncle ________________________________.

e. The car ________________________________.

f. The team ________________________________.

8. Rewrite the story below, replacing the underlined naming words with other naming words that can be used in their place.

On Alisha's birthday, Mum and Dad asked Alisha what Alisha wanted to do. Alisha said that Alisha would like to go to an amusement park. Mum and Dad agreed and Mum and Dad took Alisha and her younger brother Jai to the amusement park. Jai wanted to go on the roller coaster, but Mum told Jai that Jai must wait a few more years before Jai could take a ride on the roller coaster. Alisha asked Dad to come with Alisha on the roller coaster and Dad agreed. After the ride was over, Mum asked Alisha where Dad was. Alisha pointed at a man sitting on a bench, holding his head. The ride was too scary for Dad!

____

____

____

____

____

____

____

____

____

____

____

ISBN 978-93-5103-600-5

9. Fill in the blanks with **me**, **us**, **him** or **them** to complete the story.

My brother and I were lost in the forest. We were tired and hungry. I sat down and started to cry. My brother hugged ________ and said, "Don't worry, I'm sure we shall find a way out soon!"

Suddenly, we heard birds singing high up in the trees. I tugged at my brother's arm and pointed at two big birds with colourful feathers. They saw ________ and flew down. Then, right before our eyes, they turned into two people, dressed like a king and a queen.

I looked at my brother and whispered to ________, "Should we ask ________ for help?"

The queen smiled kindly and said, "Come, follow ________!" The king and queen turned back into birds and flew through the forest. We followed ________ and were soon out of the forest.

"Thank you!" we said and waved to ________ as they flew back into the forest.

Spot the Error

10. There is a mistake in each sentence. Underline it and rewrite the sentence correctly in the blank below.

a. I shall celebrate diwali at my aunt's house this year.

____

b. The bus stopped and two ladys got on.

____

c. The vixen and his cubs live in a den.

____

d. Are you sure this is Kunals bag?

____

e. If your parents are at home, I would like to speak with him.

____

 ISBN 978-93-5103-600-5

4 A, An and The

Let's Recall

- We use **a**, **an** and **the** to introduce a naming word.
- We use **a** or **an** to talk about one person, animal or thing.
- We use **a** when the first letter of the naming word is not a vowel.
- We use **an** when the first letter of the naming word is a vowel.
- We use **the** for a particular thing and for anything that is the only one of its kind.

4.1 Revising a, an, the

1. Look at the pictures below. Write the name of each fruit in the correct box.

a	an
____________	____________
____________	____________
____________	____________
____________	____________

2. Fill in each blank below with **a**, **an** or **the**.

a.  ______ moon

b.  ______ aeroplane

c.  ______ fish

d.  ______ elephant

3. Circle the correct word to complete each sentence below.

a. Neeta won't lie. She is (a / an) honest girl.

b. I could see two aeroplanes in (a / the) sky.

c. The pirate was very grumpy because he had (an / a) headache.

d. Aunt Maggie bought (an / a) umbrella at the new mall.

Take Note
In some words, the first letter is silent, so we hear a vowel sound when we say them. We use **an** before these words, e.g. **an** hour.

 ISBN 978-93-5103-600-5

4.2 The

Read the story.

Dad sits down on **the** armchair and reads a newspaper. Some children are playing outside.

Dad stops reading **the** newspaper because there is too much noise.

Mum tells **the** children to play quietly.

What are the children playing? What will they do now?

What is Dad reading?

Where does Dad sit?

Who are making noise?

1. Note the highlighted words in the story above. Write two common names mentioned twice.

   a. ________________ b. ________________

2. Fill in the blanks with **a**, **an** or **the**. The pictures will help you.

   a. Mum made ________  of lemonade for the children. She put ________  with ________  of nuts on a table on the lawn.

   b. ________  saw ________  of nuts and ran towards it.

   c. Mum saw ________  and jumped up on ________ , screaming. She thought it was ________ .

   d. Dad helped Mum to climb down from ________ . Everyone had a good laugh!

The is used before a naming word that has been mentioned earlier. It is also used before a naming word for something that is the only one you can see.

  ISBN 978-93-5103-600-5

Let's Practise

A. Read the note Sheena received from her grandmother and colour the correct cake below.

Dear Sheena,

Please go to the bakery to collect a cake for me. **The** cake that I want has strawberries on top. You must look for one that is square, with chocolate sprinkles on **the** sides. Please don't buy **the** cake that has words or candles on it. Thank you!

Love,
Grandma

B. Match the columns below.

1.	Grandfather bought me an ice cream. •	• a.	In **the** dream, I was chased by aliens!
2.	I had a strange dream last night. •	• b.	**The** ice cream was so cold and creamy.
3.	Uncle Tom gave me a book last summer. •	• c.	I keep my earrings in **the** pot.
4.	Mum taught me how to paint a pot. •	• d.	**The** book was about Egypt.

C. Fill in each blank below with **a**, **an** or **the**.

1. We are going out for ________ walk.
2. ________ woman with curly hair is my mother.
3. Wow! ________ ice-cream cake Aunt Jenny bought is really good.
4. I have never travelled on ________ aeroplane before.
5. I sat on ________ chair in the corner.

 ISBN 978-93-5103-600-5

5 Describing Words

Let's Recall

- Everything around us has a name. These names are called **naming words**.
- Words that tell us more about naming words are called **describing words**.

5.1 Revising describing words

1. Underline the **describing words** and circle the **naming words** they describe in the sentences below.

   a. Uncle bought a new bicycle.

   b. The strong boy helped the old man push the cart.

   c. We washed the dirty dishes after dinner.

   d. The scary film made the children cry.

2. Match each **describing word** with a picture of the **naming word**.

   a. green •   • i. 

   b. grey •   • ii. 

   c. dark •   • iii. 

   d. yellow •   • iv. 

Take Note
Describing words can tell us about the shape, size and colour of naming words.

3. Fill in each blank with the correct **describing word** from the box below.

thin	tall	short	little

   a. In winter, the days are ________ and the nights are long.

   b. David is a ________ boy even though he eats a lot.

   c. The lion laughed at the ________ mouse because it looked so weak.

   d. Mohini is a very ________ girl. In fact, everyone in school is shorter than her.

 ISBN 978-93-5103-600-5

5.2 Position of describing words

Read the story.

Aunt Denise looked **pretty** in her gown.

The wedding ring she got was **shiny** and **beautiful**.

Her dinner party was **great**. Everyone was **happy**.

Do you think the guests enjoyed themselves? How can you tell?

How did Aunt Denise look in her wedding gown?

How did the ring look?

How was the dinner party?

1. Look at the example sentence below. Write your own sentences about the story above using the describing words and naming words given below.

Describing word + Naming word	→	Sentence
Example shiny ring	→	The ring is shiny.
a. pretty gown	→	
b. great party	→	
c. happy people	→	

2. Fill in each blank with a describing word with the help of the picture given.

a. The car breaks down easily because it is ________  .

b. The children are ________  because it is past their bedtime.

c. Reena is ________  because she has won the first prize.

Describing words are not always placed before naming words. They can also be placed after the words **is/was** and **are/were**.

 ISBN 978-93-5103-600-5

Let's Practise

A. Fill in each blank with a **describing word** using the picture given.

1. These apples are ________. 

2. Abdul is ________ but his grandmother is ________. 

3. The elephant's trunk is ________. 

B. Fill in the crossword puzzle below with the correct **describing words**. The clues will help you. One has been done for you.

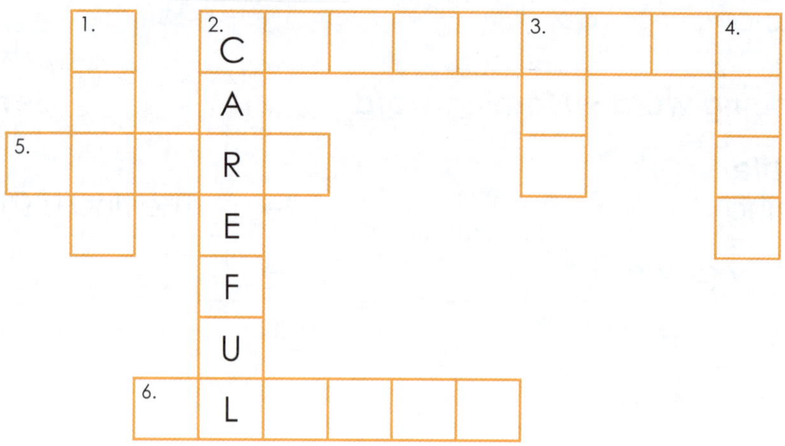

Across

2. Those kites look so bright and _____ against the blue sky.
5. Her parents are _____ because she lied to them.
6. He was _____ and could hardly keep his eyes open in class.

Down

1. My mother is _____ and cares for us a lot.
2. Mary was _____ and checked her answers before handing in her work.
3. My bag is _____ and my lunch box is the same colour.
4. The music is so _____ that I cannot hear you talk.

Think & Share Pair up with a classmate. Make sentences with the same describing word. In the first sentence use it before a naming word, and in the second sentence use it after the words **is/was/are/were**. Compare your sentences.

 ISBN 978-93-5103-600-5

5.3 How many?

Read the story.

Can you see **four** foxes playing in the grass?

Can you see **two** caterpillars on the leaves? **One** butterfly flies close by.

Can you see **eight** tadpoles in the pond? **Two** frogs are sitting on a lily pad.

How many kinds of babies can you see? What are these babies called?

How many foxes are playing in the grass?

How many caterpillars are on the leaves?

How many tadpoles are in the pond?

1. Unscramble the words that tell us how many animals there are in the sentences in the pictures above.

a. OFUR foxes ________ c. NEO butterfly ________

b. WOT caterpillars ________ d. GEIHT tadpoles ________

2. Fill in each blank with a word that tells us how many people or things there are. The picture will help you.

a. That building has ____________ storeys.

b. There are ____________ cherries on the plate.

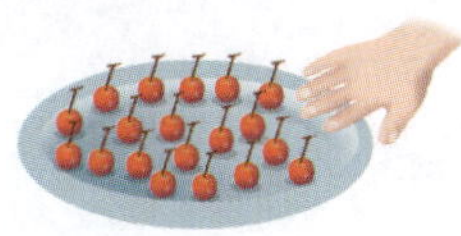

c. There are ____________ goldfish in the bowl.

d. There are ____________ rabbits in the meadow.

Numbers are also describing words. They tell us how many people, places, animals or things there are.

 ISBN 978-93-5103-600-5

Let's Practise

A. Fill in the boxes with the help of the clues below to show how many. The circled letters will answer the question given below.

1. Earth has ____ moon.
2. A year has ____ months.
3. We have ____ fingers on each hand.
4. A rainbow has ____ colours.
5. The Indian flag has ____ stripes.
6. Ten minus one is ____.

How many players are there in a cricket team? ________

B. Complete the story using describing words that are **numbers**. Then make a drawing in the box for your story.

Suman and Sudhir live in a small hut by the river. One day, there is a big storm. The strong winds destroy two trees by the riverbank ...

 ISBN 978-93-5103-600-5

5.4 Comparison

Read the story.

"Should I make this picture **bigger** for Grandmother?" asks Jim. "No, I want a **nicer** picture of your father," says Mum.

"How about this one? Dad is smiling," says Mum. "I know one where you look **more beautiful**!" says Jim.

"I think we should choose this one. We look **happier**!" says Mum.

Who do you think are in the picture? Do you have a family picture?

What did Jim offer to do?

Which picture of Mum did Jim want to choose?

Why did Mum choose the last picture?

1. Fill in each blank with a suitable word from the story above.

   a. A cat is ____________ than a mouse. 

   b. Sudha's dress is nice but Tina's dress is ____________.

   c. The view from this window is beautiful but that window's view is ____________. 

2. Underline the describing words below.

   Grandmother loved the picture Mum sent. "The children look taller!" she thought. "Jim's hair is curlier and Vinny looks lovelier! I thought Vera's hair would be longer by now. The only thing that is longer is Tim's moustache!"

To **compare** naming words, we often add **-r** or **-er** to their describing words. For describing words ending in **-y**, we replace the **-y** with **-ier**. For longer describing words, such as beautiful or thoughtful, we add **more** before the describing word. We often also add **than** after the describing word.

 ISBN 978-93-5103-600-5

Let's Practise

A. Fill in each blank with the opposite **describing word** from the box below. The pictures will help you.

happier	bigger	taller	louder

Take Note
For some describing words, the last letter is doubled before adding **-er**, e.g. **thin + n + er = thinner**.

I am **smaller** than you.	1.	I am ______________ than you.
I am **shorter** than you.	2.	I am ______________ than you.
I am **sadder** than you.	3.	I am ______________ than you.
My music is **softer** than yours.	4.	My music is ______________ than yours.

B. Write the correct form of each **describing word** to show **comparison**.

1. long ______________
2. strong ______________
3. fat ______________
4. wet ______________
5. sad ______________
6. difficult ______________

C. Fill in each blank with the correct **describing word** from the box below. The picture will help you.

smaller	taller	bigger	more playful

1. The giraffe is ______________ than the lion. 
2. The cat is ______________ than the elephant. 
3. The flower is ______________ than the mouse. 
4. Rabbits are ______________ than sheep. 

 ISBN 978-93-5103-600-5

5.5 My, our, your, his, her, its, their

Read the story.

It was raining. I took out **my** umbrella and held it by **its** handle. Mary put on **her** raincoat.

Ben and Henry did not have umbrellas. Ben used **his** bag to cover **their** heads.

Mum said, "Take off **your** wet shoes." We took off **our** wet clothes and shoes quickly!

What do you think happened next?

What did Mary put on?

What did Ben use to cover his head?

What did Mum say to the children?

1. Fill in each blank with a word from the story above.

a. Ria wants to make a vase for ________ mother with some clay.

b. ________ brother is at ________ music class.

c. My dog played in the mud and got ________ fur dirty.

2. Circle the correct word to complete each sentence below.

a. Mr Murthy bought lots of gifts for his children. They opened (our / their) gifts happily.

b. Mum says that we must clean up (our / its) room this weekend.

c. Finish (your / our) homework so we can play.

We use **my**, **our**, **your**, **his**, **her**, **its** and **their** with naming words to show that they belong to someone or something.

 ISBN 978-93-5103-600-5

Let's Practise

A. Match each bag to its correct owner.

1. **My** bag has flowers on it.

2. **Our** bag is round.

3. **My** bag is shaped like a guitar.

4. **My** bag has triangles on it.

a. 

b. 

c. 

d. 

B. Fill in the blanks below with **his**, **her** or **their**. The picture will help you.

Lots of people have brought ________ pets for the pet show. Miss Johnson was the first to arrive this morning. The blue parrot is ________ pet. Nakul is here too. ________ puppy is running around in circles. Ila has just arrived. She has a puppy too. ________ puppy's fur is brown. I like Mr Roger's pets the most. ________ green snakes are beautiful!

Think & Share Pair up with a classmate. Describe your house while your partner draws the details. Use words such as **my**, **our** and **its** in your description. After the drawing is complete, your partner has to describe the drawing using words such as **your** and **its**.

 ISBN 978-93-5103-600-5

6 Doing Words

Let's Recall

- Words that tell us what a person, an animal or a thing does are called **doing words.**
- The doing word is different when it is used for one thing and when it is used for many things. For example, Raj **plays** in the park every evening. Raj, Sam and Sona **play** together.
- The words **is**, **am** and **are** are different ways of saying **be**.
- The words **is**, **am** and **are** can also be helping words. We use them with other doing words.
- A doing word that comes after **is**, **am** or **are** often ends with **-ing**.
- We use the words **has** and **have** to show that something belongs to someone or some other thing.

6.1 Revising doing words

1. Unscramble each **doing word**. Write it in the blank below. The picture will help you.

a.  tae ________

b.  ylap ________

c.  wtire ________

d.  evid ________

 ISBN 978-93-5103-600-5

2. Circle the **be words** in the sentences below.

a. We are not teenagers.
b. This is a clever robot.
c. They are music teachers.
d. She is a tall girl.
e. I am a proud Indian.
f. A potato is a vegetable.

3. Fill in each blank below with **is**, **am** or **are**.

a. It ________ hot in summer.
b. There ________ five sparrows sitting on the branch.
c. I ________ from Rajasthan.
d. You ________ an excellent cook.
e. This ________ a good place to hide.
f. I ________ the class monitor.

4. Fill in each blank below with **is**, **am** or **are**. The picture will help you.

a. The box ________ red.

b. The book ________ orange.

c. The buildings ________ tall.

d. The butterflies ________ pretty.

5. Fill in each blank by adding **-ing** to a suitable **doing word** from the box below.

pack	plant	walk	jump	land	learn

a. Pam is ________________ sunflower seeds.
b. You are ________________ your schoolbag.
c. The children are ________________ in a straight line.
d. The pilot is ________________ the aeroplane.
e. I am ________________ French.
f. The frogs are ________________ near the pond.

 ISBN 978-93-5103-600-5

6. Look at the pictures below. Make a sentence about each using a **doing word** and **-ing**.

a. ______________________________

b. ______________________________

c. ______________________________

d. ______________________________

7. Help the frog cross the river. It can only use stones that have **doing words** in them. Colour those stones.

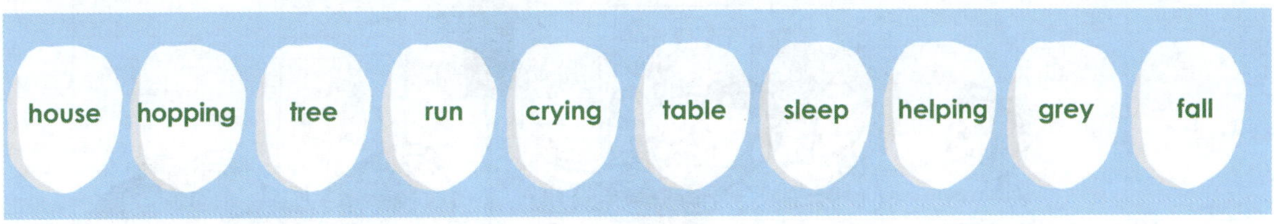

8. Fill in each blank below with **has** or **have**.

a. The cat ________ black eyes.

b. The butterflies ________ colourful wings.

c. My friend and I ________ many toy cars.

d. The boy ________ beads in his hand.

e. Mr James ________ three parrots.

f. I ________ a friend named Jaya.

 ISBN 978-93-5103-600-5

9. Look at the pictures below. Write sentences with **has** for pictures that show one naming word. Write sentences with **have** for pictures that show more than one naming word.

Example The Indian flag has four colours.

a.  ______________________

b.  ______________________

c.  ______________________

d.  ______________________

10. Look at the picture below. Write five sentences about it using **has** and **have**.

____

____

____

____

____

 ISBN 978-93-5103-600-5

6.2 Was, were

Read the story.

We **were** at the circus on Sunday. We **were** so excited!

There **was** a clown. He made us laugh with his funny tricks!

There **was** a tightrope walker too. She walked on a rope high above us. She **was** very clever!

Have you ever been to a circus? What did you see?

Where was the family on Sunday?

What did the clown do?

What did the tightrope walker do?

Remember!
The words **is**, **am** and **are** are different ways of saying **be**. **Be** tells us who someone is or what something is.

1. Read the story again. Circle the correct word to complete each sentence below.

   a. It (was / were) a Sunday, so the family decided to go to the circus.

   b. There (was / were) many people at the circus.

   c. The boy (was / were) happy to see the clown's tricks.

   d. The people (was / were) excited to see the tightrope walker.

2. Fill in each blank with a word from the story above.

   a. I ________ at the park yesterday.

   b. Maya ________ happy to see her grandmother.

   c. We ________ in the garden this morning when it began to rain.

   d. The monkeys ________ in the tree, eating bananas.

   e. The book ________ on the table.

Was and **were** are also forms of **be**. When we talk about something that happened in the past, we use **was** and **were**.

 ISBN 978-93-5103-600-5

Let's Practise

A. Match the columns with the help of the pictures given.

1.	I was		a.	a great man.
2.	He was		b.	a pretty little bird.
3.	She was		c.	late to work again today.
4.	It was		d.	happy because her best friend was coming over.
5.	Mahatma Gandhi was		e.	asleep when the phone rang.

B. Complete each sentence with the correct words from the box below.

The birds were	You were	We were

1. ____________ ahead of me in the line for the bus.

2. ____________ at the ticket counter of the amusement park.

3. ____________ on the branches of the old tree.

C. Circle the correct word to complete each sentence below.

1. (I / You) was scared when the lights went off.
2. (They / I) were very tired after the picnic.
3. (We / She) were delighted when we won the prize.
4. (They / It) was late when Matt got home.

Take Note

We use **was** with the words **I**, **he**, **she** and **it** and with naming words for one person, place, animal or thing. We use **were** with the words **we**, **you** and **they** and with naming words for more than one person, place, animal or thing.

 ISBN 978-93-5103-600-5

6.3 Had

Read the story.

Romir **had** coffee with Sara every Sunday.

The café was busy. They **had** a long wait.

Finally, it was time to order. The waiter **had** a big smile!

What do you think Romir and Sara ordered at the café?

Why did Romir go to the café?

What happened at the café?

How did the waiter look?

1. Match the columns to make complete sentences about the story above.

a.	The café	•	•	i. had a long wait.
b.	The waiter	•	•	ii. had green trousers.
c.	Romir	•	•	iii. had many customers.
d.	Romir and Sara	•	•	iv. had a writing pad.

Remember!
We use the words **has** and **have** to show that something belongs to someone or some other thing.

2. Circle the word that can be replaced with the word **had**. Then rewrite each sentence below using **had**.

   a. Lisa has a headache.

   ____

   b. We have a lot of homework.

   ____

   c. The cat has a sore paw.

   ____

   d. The chairs have broken legs.

   ____

We use **had** to show that something belonged to someone or some other thing in the past. We use it for things that happened to people or affected them. We also use **had** to say what we ate or drank. **Had** is followed by naming words.

 ISBN 978-93-5103-600-5

Let's Practise

A. Fill in each blank below with **has**, **have** or **had**.

1. We ________ lunch at school every day.
2. Peter can't come with us on New Year's Day. He ________ a party then.
3. Mona ________ short hair when she was little.
4. We ________ a music class on Fridays.
5. Agra ________ many beautiful forts.
6. I ________ a sandwich for lunch yesterday.

B. Complete each sentence using **has**, **have** or **had**. The picture will help you.

1. The cats ________________________________

2. A sunflower ________________________________

3. Yesterday, Ron ________________________________

C. Draw a star for each sentence that says that something belonged to someone in the past. Draw a circle for each sentence that talks about something that happened in the past.

1. We had a black car last year. ☐
2. Sanya's class had a picnic at Lodhi Gardens on Saturday. ☐
3. The girls had a tennis match yesterday. ☐
4. Priya had long hair last year. Now it is short! ☐
5. I had a nightmare last night. ☐

Think & Share Make three groups. Each group gets a word, **has**, **have** or **had**. Each group makes five sentences with their word. The other two groups then change the sentences using the word given to them. Share the sentences with the whole class to show the change.

 ISBN 978-93-5103-600-5

6.4 More about doing words

Read the story.

Jessie **paints** imaginary creatures. She **painted** many pictures during the holidays.

Her family **loves** her paintings. They **loved** the painting of the alien the most.

She **dreams** about her paintings before she makes them. She **dreamed** the alien and she were friends.

What do you think Jessie will draw next?

What does Jessie like to do? What did she do in the holidays?

What does her family think about her paintings?

What did Jessie dream?

Take Note
We can also write **dreamed** as **dreamt**.

1. From the story above, circle the correct doing word to complete each sentence.

   a. Jessie (paints / painted) an alien during the holidays.

   b. Jessie (loves / loved) painting pictures.

   c. Last night Jessie (dreams / dreamed) that the alien and she were friends.

2. Look at each picture. In the blank below, write a doing word to show the action happened in the past.

   a.  ________

   b.  ________

   c.  ________

   d.  ________

We use the doing word as it is for actions as they happen. We add **-d** or **-ed** to the doing word for actions that happened in the past.

 ISBN 978-93-5103-600-5

Let's Practise

A. Rewrite each sentence by changing the **doing word** to show that it happened in the past.

1. We race to the playground at lunchtime.

   ____

2. My grandmother visits us in the winter.

   ____

3. The cat climbs over the fence.

   ____

4. Simon cleans his car at the weekend.

   ____

5. My sister bakes a cake on my birthday.

   ____

6. I walk to the market to buy fruit.

   ____

B. Look at the picture below. Fill in the blanks with the correct **doing words**.

Ria's family went on a holiday. The children ________ their bags the night before. The next morning, the taxi ________. Ria ran down and got into the car. Her brother Ratan ________ Dad to put the bags in the car. Dad ________ all the heavy ones carefully because he was afraid of hurting his back. Mum ________ the door. Dad ________ to see that everything was in place. "Hurray! We are off at last," said Ria.

 ISBN 978-93-5103-600-5

7 How Words

Let's Recall

- Everything around us has a name. These names are called **naming words**.
- Words that tell us more about naming words are called **describing words**.
- Words that tell us what a person, an animal or a thing does are called **doing words**.

7.1 Revising naming, describing and doing words

1. Sort the words by writing them on the correct book.

flowers	bright	knock	listen	cloud	strong
sweet	jumped	Monday			

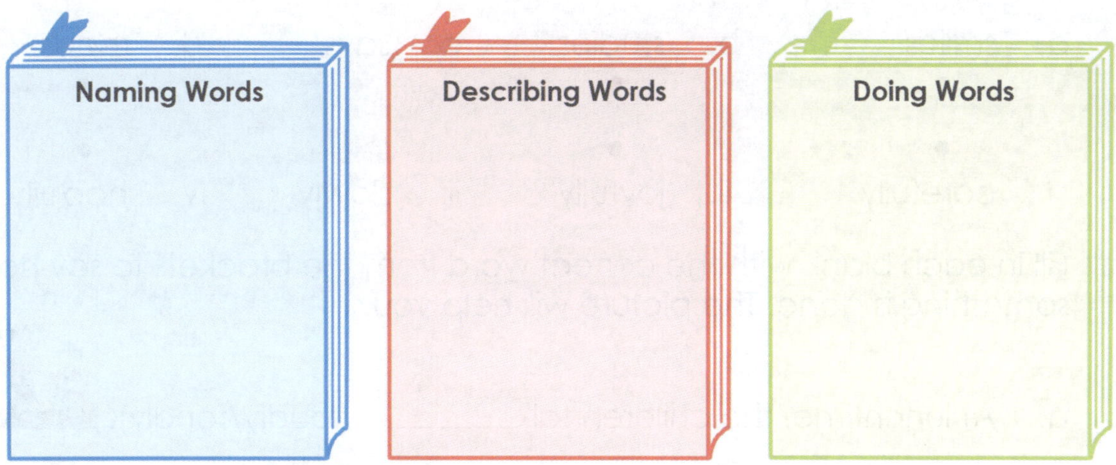

2. Fill in each blank with a **doing word**.

   a. Sharks ________ in the ocean.

   b. Suma ________ a cake for Mum's birthday last week.

   c. Grandmother ________ me a story at bedtime.

   d. The bird ________ into my garden every morning.

   e. They ________ all the way to school.

 ISBN 978-93-5103-600-5

7.2 What are how words?

Read the story.

Ryan has an English test tomorrow. He studies for his test **carefully**.

Ryan reads the questions **slowly**. He then writes the answers **neatly**.

He sees his marks and smiles **happily**. "Excellent work!" says Dad **joyfully**.

How do you think Ryan did in his test?

How does Ryan study?

How does he write his answers?

How does he smile?

1. From the story above, match each doing word with the word that describes it.

a. smiles	b. studies	c. says	d. reads
•	•	•	•
•	•	•	•
i. carefully	ii. joyfully	iii. slowly	iv. happily

2. Fill in each blank with the correct word from the brackets to say how something is done. The picture will help you.

a. At lunchtime, the children talk ________ (loudly/fondly). 

b. The sun is shining ________ (brightly/clearly). 

c. Rishabh dances ________ (sadly/happily) to his favourite song. 

d. The shopkeeper shouted ________ (angrily/sweetly) at the salesman. 

Some words tell us how something is done. They usually end with **-ly**.

 ISBN 978-93-5103-600-5

Let's Practise

A. Fill in each blank with a suitable word from the box below. Add **-ly** to show how the action is done.

quiet	quick	loud	soft

1. The baby cried ________ when he lost the balloon.

2. Cheetahs can run very ________.

3. In the library, everyone reads ________.

4. The thief walked ________ so no one heard him.

B. Find six words that end in **-ly** in the word grid below.

Q	F	G	B	L	O	P	D	S	S
E	R	S	A	V	C	R	Z	C	X
P	E	A	C	E	F	U	L	L	Y
N	M	D	P	I	O	I	U	E	T
F	Q	L	G	T	N	J	H	V	X
G	W	Y	V	R	D	L	K	E	C
N	E	S	B	D	L	M	B	R	V
S	L	O	W	L	Y	R	T	L	H
R	B	C	L	E	A	R	L	Y	G
R	T	Y	U	E	W	D	F	S	Q

Take Note
We can often turn a describing word into a how word by adding **-ly** at the end, e.g. **quick** + **ly** = **quickly**.

Think & Share Pair up with a classmate and make a list of doing words. Take turns to suggest **-ly** words that say how the action is done, for example, sing – sweetly.

 ISBN 978-93-5103-600-5

Review 2

1. Fill in each blank below with **a**, **an** or **the**.

   a. Mum gave me ________ orange for breakfast. 
   ________ orange was sour!

   b. Last week, Jeremy and his friends saw ________ film. 
   ________ film was about ________ lost dog.

   c. Once upon a time, ________ old, wise man lived in ________ quiet village. 

   d. ________ girl riding ________ bicycle is my sister. 

   e. Do you know ________ lady who has four cats? She loves animals. 

2. Fill in each blank below with a **describing word**.

   a. My bicycle is ________.
   b. Lily's dress is so ________!
   c. The baby is ________.
   d. The teapot is ________.

3. Underline the **describing words** that show how many.

   Simi is working on her school project. She takes out one sheet of chart paper. She draws four columns. Then she divides the columns into six rows each. She uses five colours to write on her chart. She sticks on pictures of ten animals.

4. Look at the words given in the brackets. Change them to show **comparison** between the people or things in the sentences below.

   a. I am ____________ (short) than my brother.
   b. A blue whale is ____________ (heavy) than twenty-five elephants.
   c. Good health is ____________________ (important) than money.
   d. Skateboarding is ____________________ (dangerous) than cricket.

 ISBN 978-93-5103-600-5

5. Rewrite the sentences below using **his**, **her**, **its** or **their** in place of the underlined words.

Example This is Tanvi's football.

This is her football.

a. These are Alvin and Lucy's crayons.

____

b. This is Mr Anwar's handwriting.

____

c. Kate is a photographer. This is Kate's camera.

____

d. Kapil is Kumaran's friend.

____

e. Sujit has a cat named Tabby. Tabby's eyes are blue.

____

6. Fill in each blank below with **my**, **your** or **our**.

a. My name is Arya, and this is ________ sketchbook.

b. We are cricketers, and these are ________ bats.

c. You are a musician. Is that ________ guitar?

d. ________ family loves noodles. We often cook noodles at home.

e. You must all wipe ________ shoes before coming into the house.

f. We have to go to the parent-teacher meeting at school with ________ parents.

7. Circle the correct word to complete each sentence below.

a. Ajay and Patrick (was / were) absent from class yesterday.

b. The weather (was / were) fine yesterday evening.

c. Cora (was / were) in the garden when the telephone rang.

d. The Maths and English tests (was / were) very easy.

e. I (was / were) born in November.

f. These shoes (was / were) comfortable before, but now they seem too tight.

 ISBN 978-93-5103-600-5

8. Fill in each blank below with **has**, **have** or **had**.

a. The zoo ________ many kinds of animals.

b. How many pairs of shoes do you ________?

c. Rahul ________ only twenty minutes to complete his test yesterday.

d. Riya and Aisha ________ the same hairstyle.

e. I ________ a milkshake for breakfast today.

9. Read each sentence below. In the blank, write **Now** if the doing word is for an action as it happens or **Before** if the doing word is for an action that happened in the past.

a. I talked to Uncle Ben last week. ________

b. Sheena walks to school. ________

c. Raj plays the guitar. ________

d. Jessie's family travelled to Agra by train. ________

10. Fill in the crossword with words that tell us about something that happened in the past. The clues below will help you.

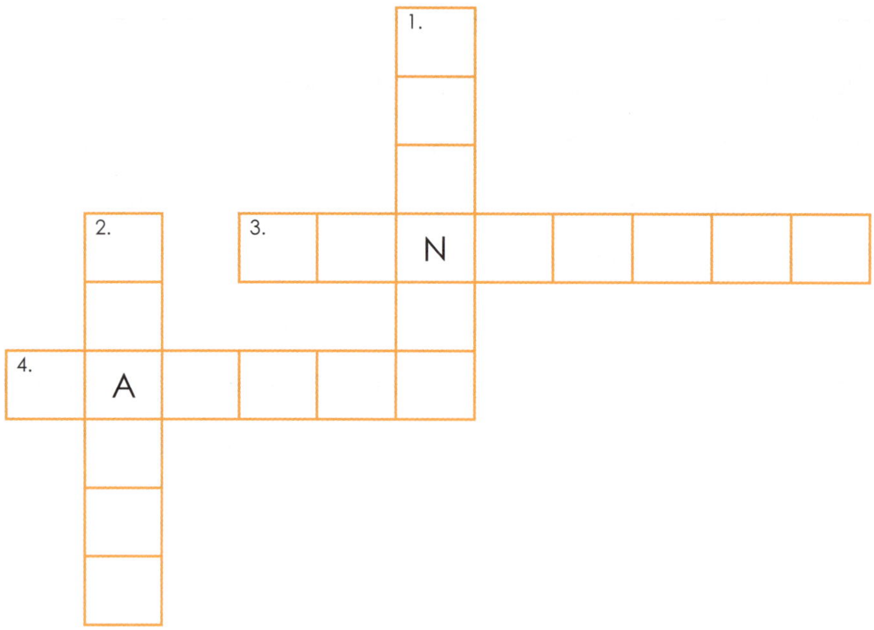

Across

3. I ____ my homework, then went to the playground.

4. The dog ____ when the phone rang at night.

Down

1. I ____ the door and found my favourite uncle standing outside.

2. The little girl ____ the piano beautifully.

 ISBN 978-93-5103-600-5

11. Add **-ly** to each word below and use it in a sentence to say how something is done. The pictures will help you.

Example loud: The lion roared loudly.

a. slow: ____________________ 

b. nervous: ____________________ 

c. playful: ____________________ 

d. sad: ____________________ 

Spot the Error

12. There is a mistake in each sentence. Underline it and rewrite the sentence correctly in the blank below.

a. There is the fence around our garden.

____

b. A man with a walking stick is my grandfather.

____

c. A cat is more smart than a dog.

____

d. The children packed away its toys.

____

e. When I reached home, I found the lock were broken.

____

f. This bakery always have fresh bread and cakes.

____

g. I have a glass of orange juice before coming to school today.

____

h. Does you have any pets at home?

____

i. I walk home with my best friend yesterday.

____

j. She chewed her sandwich slow.

____

 ISBN 978-93-5103-600-5

8 Where Words

Let's Recall

- Everything around us has a name. These names are called **naming words**.
- Words that tell us what a person, an animal or a thing does are called **doing words**.
- Words such as **in**, **on**, **near**, **above**, **below** and **under** tell us where something or someone is. They are called **where words**.

8.1 Revising where words

1. Underline the incorrect **where word** in each sentence below. Write the correct where word in the blank next to it. The picture will help you.

   a. Varun put all the waste paper under the bin. ________ 

   b. The crow finds a pot of water on a tree. ________ 

   c. Grandfather put the kettle in the stove. ________ 

   d. When the nights are cold, my dog quietly slips above my blanket. ________ 

2. Fill in each blank with the correct **where word**. The picture will help you.

   a. Ria likes to sit ________ the window in class. 

   b. Nina stands ________ a stool and brushes her teeth. 

   c. The colourful ball is ________ the desk. 

   d. The blue birds sit ________ the yellow ones on the tree. 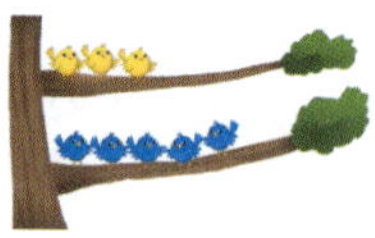

   e. The chef put some salt ________ the pan. 

   f. We switch on the bright lamp ________ the table at dinnertime. 

 ISBN 978-93-5103-600-5

8.2 More about where words

Read the story.

Roy and his friends are **at** the sports centre **behind** his house.

On the badminton court, Roy hits the shuttlecock **over** the net.

On the football field, Roy kicks the football **into** the goal. Roy is a hero!

Does Roy like sports? Why do you think so?

Where are Roy and his friends?

What does Roy do on the badminton court?

What does he do on the football field?

1. Fill in each blank with a word from the story above.

   a. There are many children ________ the sports centre.

   b. Pam stands ________ Roy and watches him hit the shuttlecock.

   c. Roy's friends watch him kick the football ________ their heads.

2. Circle the correct word to complete each sentence below. The picture will help you.

   a. The giraffe is standing (by / over) the elephant.

   b. Naina got (into / behind) the taxi quickly.

   c. Mum will come back (by / from) the market soon.

Words such as **at, by, from, over, into** and **behind** tell us where something or someone is. They are known as **where words**.

 ISBN 978-93-5103-600-5

Let's Practise

A. Fill in the blanks with the correct **where words** from the box to complete the story. You may use some words more than once. The picture will help you.

by	at	over	into	from	behind

There was a robbery ________ Mrs Verma's house on Saturday. Mrs Verma was not ________ home when it happened. Police say the robber jumped ________ the fence ________ the apple tree. They found muddy marks ________ the fence. The thief came ________ her house and ate cookies ________ the jar in the kitchen. Police found a small red collar with "Fluffy" written on it ________ a curtain in the room.

B. Fill in each blank below with a suitable **where word**.

1. I turned around and saw Sam standing ________ me in the line.
2. My school is ________ the end of this road.
3. The helicopter flew ________ the cloud.
4. There is a mango tree ________ the lake.
5. On a hot day, I cannot wait to jump ________ the pool.
6. The magician took out a parrot ________ his hat.

Think & Share Pair up with a classmate to play "Where is it?". Hide an object somewhere in your classroom. Give your partner clues using where words, such as "It is **by** a window" or "It is **under** a chair" to help them find the object. Swap roles and repeat with another object.

 ISBN 978-93-5103-600-5

9 Joining Words

Let's Recall

- A **sentence** is a group of words that makes complete sense.
- We use the word **and** to join two sentences together. It is called a **joining word**.

9.1 Revising joining words

1. Match the sentences and join them using **and**. Write the joined sentences in the blanks below.

a.	Irfan opened his schoolbag.	i.	He buys fresh fruit and vegetables.
b.	The sun is shining.	ii.	She put the apple in her basket.
c.	Samuel goes to the market every day.	iii.	He took out his books.
d.	Kavita picked an apple from the tree.	iv.	There are no clouds in the sky.

2. Look at the picture below and write three sentences about it using **and**.

 ISBN 978-93-5103-600-5

9.2 And, or, but

Read the story.

"Who can help with weeding **and** watering the school garden?" asks Mrs Dawson.

"I can help on Monday **or** Tuesday," says Meg. "I love being outdoors!"

"I would like to help, **but** I shall be on holiday next week," says Sam.

Where do you think Sam will go for his holiday?

What does Mrs Dawson need helpers for?

On which days does Meg offer to help?

Why can't Sam help out?

1. Fill in each blank with a word from the story above.

   a. Mrs Dawson needs two helpers, ________ only one child can help.

   b. Mrs Dawson needs help with weeding ________ watering.

   c. Meg can't help every day, ________ she can help on Monday ________ Tuesday.

2. Rewrite each pair of sentences below as one.

   a.  Would you like to fly a kite? Would you like to read?

   ____

   b.  I go to sleep early. I wake up early.

   ____

   c.  I want Liam to win the match. I think he is going to lose.

   ____

Joining words such as **and**, **or** and **but** are used to join words, groups of words or sentences together.

 ISBN 978-93-5103-600-5

Let's Practise

A. Underline the incorrect **joining word** in each sentence below. Then rewrite the sentence correctly. The picture will help you.

1. The hill was steep or I was able to climb it in the end.

____

2. We can order Chinese food but Italian food for dinner.

____

3. The tortoise was slower than the hare or still won the race.

____

4. Would you like tea but coffee?

____

B. Match the sentences below. Join the sentences using **and**, **or** or **but** and write them in the blanks.

1.	This book is very old. •	• a.	Is it closed on Sunday?
2.	I knocked on the door. •	• b.	They do not look like each other.
3.	Mike and Kevin are twins. •	• c.	It is still my favourite.
4.	Is the pool closed on Saturday? •	• d.	I waited for Mum to open it.

____

____

____

____

Think & Share Divide the class into three groups (**and**, **or**, **but**). Each group will make an incomplete sentence using their joining word. The other two groups will have to complete the sentence in the most interesting way they can, for example, "I like you, **but** ..." "I like crocodiles too!" or "I like your food more!"

 ISBN 978-93-5103-600-5

10 Sentences

Let's Recall

- A **sentence** is a group of words that makes complete sense.
- A sentence that says something is called a **statement**.
- A sentence that asks about something is called a **question**.
- Both statements and questions begin with a **capital letter**.
- A statement ends with a **full stop** (.).
- A question ends with a **question mark** (?).

10.1 Revising sentences

1. Rearrange each set of jumbled words to make a **statement** or a **question**. Write it on the blank below. Use full stops and question marks where needed.

   a. my scratch knee on have I a

   ____

   b. my leave I where phone did

   ____

   c. during do bats the sleep day

   ____

   d. zebra the cheetah chasing is the

   ____

   e. question this answer what is the to

   ____

2. Match each sentence beginning with a suitable sentence ending.

a.	Do you know •	•	i.	is big and brown.
b.	The spider climbed •	•	ii.	standing next to Nidhi?
c.	My neighbour's dog •	•	iii.	how to play the guitar?
d.	Who is that boy •	•	iv.	for you yesterday.
e.	A letter came •	•	v.	the water spout.

 ISBN 978-93-5103-600-5

10.2 Two parts of a sentence

Read the story.

Butterflies, bees, ladybirds and ants live in my garden.

A spider weaves its web on a branch. It wants to trap insects.

Little birds sit on the garden gate. They look for insects to eat too!

Can you think of other animals you may see in a garden?

Which animals live in this garden?

What does the spider do?

Why do the birds sit on the gate?

1. Match the columns to make sentences about the story above.

a. Little birds • • i. weaves its web.

b. A spider • • ii. live in my garden.

c. Butterflies and bees • • iii. sit on the garden gate.

2. Complete the sentences with the help of the pictures given. Underline the naming words and circle the doing words in the sentences.

Remember!
Names for people, places, animals and things are **naming words**. Words that tell us what a person, an animal or a thing does are called **doing words**.

a. Nina and I ______________________

____

b. Our Maths teacher ______________________

____

c. Joan ______________________

____

A sentence has a **naming part** and a **doing part**. The naming part tells us who or what the sentence is about. The doing part tells us something about the naming part.

 ISBN 978-93-5103-600-5

Let's Practise

A. The underlined words are the **naming part** of each sentence. Replace the naming part with your own words.

1. My sister and I visit our grandmother every summer.

   ____

2. Mr Murthy comes home late every evening.

   ____

3. This storybook has a scary ending.

   ____

4. Meera's mum bought me a set of crayons before the drawing competiton.

   ____

B. Circle the **naming part** and underline the **doing part** in each sentence below.

1. Maria and I waited for a bus.
2. Mr Rao mows his lawn every Sunday.
3. My brother Sudhir is training for a marathon.
4. I can't find my library book.

Take Note
The doing part of a sentence has the doing word.

C. Look at the picture below and write four sentences about it. Write the **naming part** with a blue pencil and the **doing part** with a red pencil.

____

____

____

____

 ISBN 978-93-5103-600-5

10.3 More about sentences

Read the story.

Mr Sinha is our neighbour. **He owns** a car-service shop.

Our **car needs** a check. **We take** our car to him.

Dad goes to pick up the car. **We go** for a drive together.

Do you think the car runs smoothly now? How do you know?

Who owns the car-service shop?

Why does the family take the car to the car-service shop?

Where does the family go after the service?

1. Circle the correct doing word to complete each sentence.

   a. Mr Sinha (owns / own) a car-service shop.

   b. We (takes / take) our car for a check.

   c. Dad (go / goes) to collect the car.

   d. We (go / goes) for a drive after the check.

2. Look at each picture below. Write a sentence for it, using the correct form of the doing word given in the brackets.

   Example The student goes to school. (go) 

   a. ______________________________ (eat) 

   b. ______________________________ (ride) 

   c. ______________________________ (juggle) 

The doing word and the naming word in a sentence must match each other. We usually add **-s** to the doing word when we talk about one person or thing.

 ISBN 978-93-5103-600-5

Let's Practise

A. Circle the correct word to complete each sentence below.

1. My brothers (plays / play) football in the field.
2. You (paint / paints) so well.
3. My mother (buys / buy) fruit from the fruit vendor.
4. I (am / is) going to the playground in the evening.
5. We (sings / sing) songs on our way to school.
6. Our teacher (gives / give) us homework on Fridays.
7. You (look / looks) so beautiful today!
8. I (has / have) three sisters.
9. My parents (is / are) taking me to the doctor for a check-up.
10. You (have / has) a stain on your shirt.

Take Note
We do not add **-s** to the doing word when we use **I** and **you**.

B. Fill in the crossword using doing words with the help of the clues below.

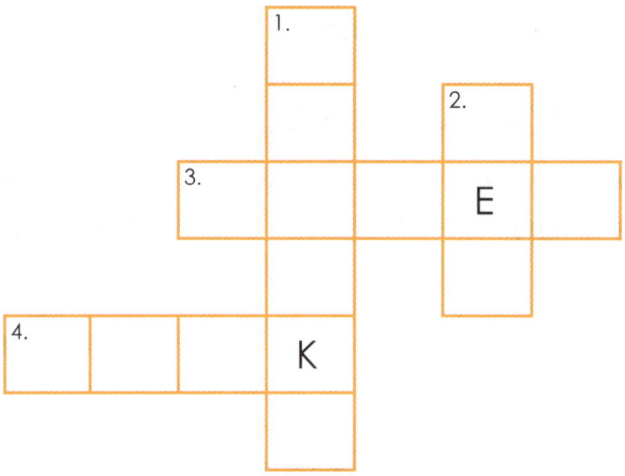

Across

3. Vibha ____ walking in the rain.
4. The builders ____ hard all day long.

Down

1. Our cat ____ milk from a special saucer.
2. Please ____ some vegetables from the market.

 ISBN 978-93-5103-600-5

10.4 Question words

Read the story.

"**Where** did the dog come from?" asks Anna.

"**How** did he get here? **What** is his name?" asks Harry.

"It's Rex. **Who** can the owner be? We must find him," says Anna.

What do you think Harry and Anna will do next?

What does Anna ask when she sees the dog?

What does Harry ask Anna?

What is the dog's name? How do you know?

1. Fill in each blank with a word from the story above.

   a. ________ do Anna and Harry find Rex?

   b. ________ do you think Rex got there?

   c. ________ does Rex belong to?

   d. ________ can Anna and Harry do to help?

2. Fill in the blanks to complete the questions below.

   a. ______ did you arrive?
   b. ______ city did you visit?
   c. ______ did you go there?
   d. ______ did you go with?

   I came back last night.
   I visited Agra.
   I went to visit my aunt.
   I went with my parents.

Sameer

Jason

We use **who, what, which, when, where, why** and **how** to ask for information. These **question words** are also known as **wh- words**.

 ISBN 978-93-5103-600-5

Let's Practise

A. Write a question using a **question word** for each answer below.

1. ______________________________

   Mr Lal is the principal of my school.

2. ______________________________

   The mail arrives in the afternoon.

3. ______________________________

   Today is 10 August.

4. ______________________________

   Anita is crying because she failed her exam.

5. ______________________________

   I opened the door with my spare key.

B. Complete the **questions** to show how Rex was lost and found. In each square, write a question to match the clue in the picture.

 ***Example*** What did Rex do when he saw the open gate?	1.  Where ______________	2.  What ______________
3.  How ______________	4.  Where ______________	5.  Why ______________

Think & Share Pair up with a classmate to play a game of "Ten Questions". Think of an animal and ask your partner to guess the name by asking questions. For example, **Where** does it live? **What** does it eat? **How** does it look? They must try to guess the correct name in ten questions.

 ISBN 978-93-5103-600-5

11 Punctuation

Let's Recall

- All sentences start with a **capital letter**.
- Special names of people, places, animals and things start with a capital letter.
- A statement ends with a **full stop** (.).
- A question ends with a **question mark** (?).

11.1 Revising capital letters, full stops and question marks

1. Rewrite the passage in your notebook with the missing **capital letters**, **full stops** and **question marks**.

   my friend anna has a new pet it is a chameleon I have so many questions for anna what is the name of the chameleon is it dangerous

   anna says her chameleon is called gizzy it is an amazing lizard it has a special tongue too its tongue is longer than its body gizzy shoots out its tongue to catch food

2. Choose a group of words from the box to complete each sentence. The pictures will help you. Use **full stops** and **question marks** where needed.

when you brush your teeth	late for school
the answer to this sum	when he showers

a. Is Vani ______________________________

b. Robbie likes to sing ______________________________

c. Who can tell me ______________________________

d. Remember to turn off the tap ______________________________

 ISBN 978-93-5103-600-5

11.2 Exclamation mark

Read the story.

Why do you think Ludo jumped up suddenly?

What did Ronnie say to Ludo when he started painting? Why?

What did he say when Ludo knocked over his paints?

What did Mum say when she looked into the room?

1. Read the story again. Then match each picture with a word.

a. 

b. 

c. 

i. Oops!

ii. Good dog!

iii. Sorry!

2. Fill in each blank below with a suitable word.

a. ________! I have hurt my knee.

b. ________! I'm stuck in the lift.

c. ________ ________! We are very proud of you!

d. ________ ________! How are you celebrating today?

We use **!** at the end of a word, a group of words or a sentence to show strong feelings, such as surprise, happiness, pain, fear or anger.

 ISBN 978-93-5103-600-5

Let's Practise

A. Match each picture with a suitable word.

1.  • • a. Wow!

2.  • • b. Hurray!

3.  • • c. Stop!

4.  • • d. Very good!

5.  • • e. Eek!

B. Replace the **.** with **!** where needed. Rewrite the sentence in the blank below.

1. Be careful.

____

2. I am at the zoo.

____

3. Stop it right now.

____

4. The test is on Friday.

____

5. Look at that beautiful rainbow.

____

6. My name is Madhu.

____

 ISBN 978-93-5103-600-5

11.3 Short forms

Read the story.

Do you think Anya and Jessie like being outdoors? How can you tell?

How does Anya introduce herself?

Who are always doing things together?

What does Anya say about Jessie?

1. Match the two columns with the help of the story above.

a.	I'm	•	•	i.	we are
b.	we're	•	•	ii.	she is
c.	she's	•	•	iii.	I am
d.	it's	•	•	iv.	he is
e.	he's	•	•	v.	it is

Remember!
We also use **'s** to show that something belongs to someone or some other thing, e.g. Sam**'s** car, a cat**'s** claws.

2. Circle the correct words to complete the story below.

This is Mr Lion and Mr Elephant. Maybe (your / you're) wondering what (they'are / they're) doing right now. (It's / Its) a way to decide who is heavier! I think Mr Elephant is heavier as (hes / he's) lower than Mr Lion on the see-saw. What do you think?

When we speak, we sometimes join some words together to make a **short form**. We write the short forms of these words by joining them with '. The ' takes the place of the missing letter or letters.

 ISBN 978-93-5103-600-5

Let's Practise

A. Read out each **short form** below. Write its full form in the blank.

1. I'm: ________
2. you're: ________
3. we're: ________
4. she's: ________
5. it's: ________
6. they're: ________

B. Fill in each blank with the **short form** of the words in the brackets.

1. (We are) ________ going on a school trip to the museum.
2. (I am) ________ meeting my best friend this evening.
3. (They are) ________ visiting our school for the first time.
4. (You are) ________ wearing my shoes!
5. (It is) ________ a good day to fly a kite.
6. (He is) ________ my cousin from Australia.

C. Look at the picture. Complete the story using the **short forms** given in the box below.

I'm she's it's we're they're

Hi, ________ Will. This is my sister Sue. ________ older than me. ________ very fond of animals. We have a dog and a mouse. ________ a sunny day today so we are giving our pets a bath. ________ clean and fresh now and want to jump around happily!

ISBN 978-93-5103-600-5

Review 3

1. Tick the correct **where words** to complete the sentences below.

   a. There is a party ____ Sneha's house.

      i. on ii. at iii. by

   b. Her house is ____ our school.

      i. near ii. under iii. into

   c. My friend Rajat will pick me up ____ my house at 4 o'clock.

      i. by ii. from iii. over

   d. Sneha will cut the birthday cake ____ her living room.

      i. on ii. by iii. in

   e. There is a small pool ____ Sneha's house.

      i. into ii. behind iii. from

   f. We shall play games ____ the pool.

      i. from ii. by iii. of

   g. Sneha said we must not jump ____ the pool.

      i. into ii. behind iii. for

   h. Sneha's parents will put a covering ____ the pool so that nobody falls in!

      i. behind ii. under iii. over

2. Fill in each blank with a **where word**. The picture will help you.

a. Ron took some beads ________ the jar.

b. The butterflies flew ________ the flowers.

c. I put some cherries ________ a cup.

d. Jason hid ________ a board.

 ISBN 978-93-5103-600-5

3. Join each pair of sentences using **or** or **but**.

a. Does Grandmother live in an old house?
Does she live in a new house?

____

____

b. The girl wanted to catch the butterfly.
She could not reach it.

____

____

c. Is the Thar Desert in Rajasthan?
Is it in Gujarat?

____

____

d. I want to learn to play the piano.
I cannot find a teacher.

____

____

e. Do you like chocolate ice cream?
Do you like vanilla ice cream?

____

____

f. I like visiting different cities.
I want to live in Mumbai.

____

____

g. We can go by bus.
We can walk.

____

____

 ISBN 978-93-5103-600-5

4. Each group of words in the red box is the **naming part** of a sentence. Each group of words in the blue box is the **doing part** of a sentence. Make suitable sentences in the blanks below by joining the naming parts and doing parts.

The three little pigs	The hungry lion	Doctors
The sky	Small pets	The peacock

looks scary.	has beautiful feathers.	turned dark.
are easy to look after.	help people who are sick.	went home.

____

____

____

____

____

____

____

5. Circle the correct doing word to complete each sentence below.

a. My dog (dig / digs) a hole in the garden every day.

b. Will you (come / comes) with me to the park this evening?

c. Mr and Mrs Patil (watches / watch) a film every Sunday.

d. Pandas (eat / eats) bamboo shoots.

e. These flowers (blooms / bloom) early in the morning.

6. Match each **question word** with a suitable ending.

a. When	•	•	i.	is a screwdriver used for?
b. Where	•	•	ii.	do we keep milk in the fridge?
c. Why	•	•	iii.	did you know I was here?
d. Which	•	•	iv.	is your house?
e. What	•	•	v.	is the school assembly?
f. Who	•	•	vi.	animal is faster?
g. How	•	•	vii.	is going with you to the park?

 ISBN 978-93-5103-600-5

7. Add (.), (**?**) or (**!**) to the sentences below.

a. Do you like watching films

b. I am scared

c. My favourite season is winter

d. Where is the ice-cream shop

e. This is yummy

f. How can I find out the answer

8. Match each **short form** with its full form.

a.	I'm	i.	we are
b.	he's	ii.	they are
c.	she's	iii.	I am
d.	it's	iv.	you are
e.	you're	v.	he is
f.	we're	vi.	she is
g.	they're	vii.	it is

Spot the Error

9. There is a mistake in each sentence. Underline it and rewrite the sentence correctly in the blank below.

a. The children jumped behind the pool.

____

b. Mohan like playing in the rain.

____

c. Why is your father?

____

d. Ouch. I have hurt my thumb.

____

e. Im brushing my teeth.

____

f. I would love to come to your party or I cannot.

____

 ISBN 978-93-5103-600-5

12 Comprehension

12.1 Similarities and differences

To understand a text better, you sometimes have to compare things in it to see how similar or different they are. This is called finding similarities and differences.

Read the description.

My Family

My name is Anu and I live in Lucknow with my parents and younger brother. My mother's name is Anita. She is tall and has short hair. She is a pilot, but she loves painting in her spare time. My father Mohit is a banker. He enjoys playing golf. He is also a great cook. My brother Udit is six years old. He goes to school with me. He loves cricket and wants to be a fast bowler. I am eight years old and I love gardening and painting. I want to be an artist when I grow up.

Take Note
A description
- often expresses the writer's feelings.
- usually uses words such as **I** and **we**.
- describes and includes details about people or places.

1. Complete the table below with information from the text.

Family member	Name	What I am	Hobby
mother			
			playing golf and cooking
me		student	
brother			

2. Tick the correct answer for each question below. The table will help you.

   a. Which two family members enjoy painting?

      i. mother and brother   ii. mother and Anu

   b. Which two family members enjoy outdoor games?

      i. father and brother   ii. mother and father

Think!
In order to find similarities and differences, you can organise the information in a table and compare each row or column.

 ISBN 978-93-5103-600-5

3. Write down one similarity and one difference between Anu and Udit.

similarity: ____

difference: ____

4. From the description, find one word that means the same as each group of words below.

a. flies a plane: ____________ b. works in a bank: ____________

5. Find three describing words in the text.

a. ____________ b. ____________ c. ____________

Let's Practise

Read the table.

My friends	Favourite colour	Favourite food	Favourite sport
Sam	red	noodles	football
Tim	blue	pizza	football
Eva	pink	pasta	basketball
Ryan	blue	noodles	badminton
Tanvi	red	pasta	cricket

A. Tick the correct answer for each question below.

1. How many friends like pizza?

   a. one b. none

2. Which friends like to play football?

   a. Sam and Tim b. Eva and Ryan

3. Which friends like the colour red?

   a. Tanvi and Sam b. Eva and Tim

4. What is common between Tim and Ryan?

   a. favourite food b. favourite colour

B. Write the names of the two friends who like noodles.

____________ and ____________

C. Write down one difference between Sam and Tim.

____

 ISBN 978-93-5103-600-5

12.2 Sequencing

To understand a text better, you try to work out the sequence of events, or the order in which things happen. This is called sequencing.

Read the explanation.

The Life Cycle of a Chicken

1. A mother hen lays eggs.
2. The mother hen sits on the eggs to keep them warm.
3. The chick feeds on the egg yolk to grow inside the egg.
4. After about twenty-one days a fuzzy baby chick hatches.
5. It grows into an adult chicken. Adult chickens begin the life cycle all over again. They can live for as long as thirty years.

Take Note
A life cycle is an explanation. An explanation
- gives some facts about a topic.
- tells the how or why about the topic.
- gives information in the order in which things happen.
- sometimes uses words such as **first**, **then**, **before** or **next**.

1. Tick the correct answer for each question below.
   a. What happens after the mother hen lays an egg?
      i. The mother hen sits on the egg.
      ii. A chick hatches.
   b. What happens after twenty-one days?
      i. A fuzzy chick comes out.
      ii. The chick feeds on the egg yolk.

Think!
In order to work out the sequence of events, you
- find the events and underline them.
- try to find out how the events are related.

2. Number the steps of the explanation to show the correct sequence.
   a. After about twenty-one days the chick is ready to hatch. ____
   b. The chick feeds on the egg yolk to grow inside the egg. ____
   c. The chick grows into an adult chicken. ____
3. From the explanation above, find one word that means the same as each group of words below.
   a. come out of an egg: ________ b. eat food: ________

 ISBN 978-93-5103-600-5

4. Write a question for each sentence below using a suitable question word.

   a. ______________________________

   A fuzzy baby chick comes out of the shell.

   b. ______________________________

   The mother hen sits on the egg to keep it warm.

Let's Practise

Read the explanation.

The Life Cycle of a Frog

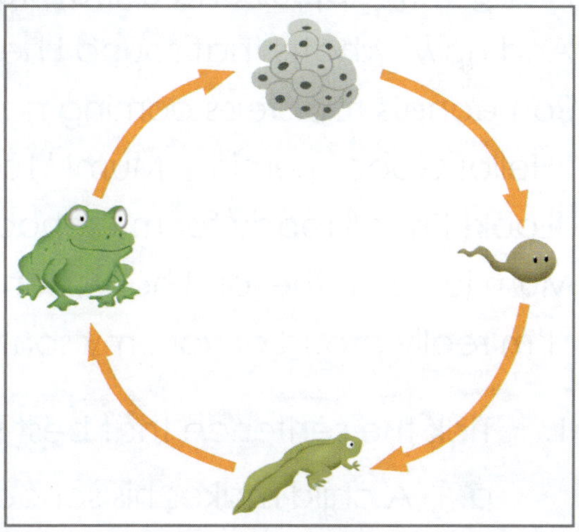

1. Frogs start their lives in water. A mother frog lays hundreds of jelly-covered eggs in the water.
2. A tiny tadpole hatches out of each egg after a few days. It has a tiny tail to help it swim to find food.
3. Slowly, the tadpole grows legs and its tail begins to shrink.
4. After some time, it develops lungs to breathe. It can now hop out of water and live on land as a froglet.
5. Soon it becomes a full-sized frog. A frog eats insects that it catches with its long sticky tongue. It also eats small fish and worms.

A. Tick the correct answer for each question below.

1. What happens first after the tadpole hatches?

   a. It develops lungs. b. It grows legs.

2. What happens after the tadpole develops lungs?

   a. It hops out of water to live on land.

   b. It becomes a full-sized frog.

B. Number the steps of the explanation to show the correct sequence.

1. The tadpole has a tiny tail to help it swim to find food. ____
2. The froglet hops out of water and lives on land. ____
3. A tiny tadpole hatches out of an egg. ____

 ISBN 978-93-5103-600-5

12.3 Summarising

To summarise a text, you give the main ideas and facts without using too many words. You need to link the important ideas and decide what the main points are. This is called summarising.

Read the poem.

A Surprise for Mum

I wake up early in the morning,
And go into the kitchen yawning!
I'll just give Mum a nice surprise,
And then she won't believe her eyes!
I pack cheese sandwiches for lunch,
Along with apples and carrots to munch!
And now, what's that sound I hear?
Someone's footsteps coming near!
"Hello! Good morning, Mum!" I say.
"Look! I'm all ready for my school day."
Mum looks at the job I have done.
"I'm really proud of you, my son!"

Take Note
A poem
- is a type of writing that shows imagination and expresses feelings.
- usually has rhyming words.

1. Tick the sentence that best summarises the poem.
   a. A child makes his school lunch to surprise his mother.
   b. A child helps his mother in the kitchen.

2. Summarise the boy's actions early in the morning.

   ____

   ____

3. From the poem above, find one word that means the opposite of each word below.
   a. late: ________ c. take: ________
   b. far: ________ d. night: ________

Think!
In order to summarise, you
- look for the main idea.
- leave out the less important details.

4. Write a suitable describing word for each naming word taken from the poem above.
   a. ________ morning c. ________ footsteps
   b. ________ job d. ________ day

 ISBN 978-93-5103-600-5

Let's Practise

Read the poem.

Woof, Wag, Woof!

My name is Cuddles,
And I love jumping in puddles.
I'm three months old,
And always sit where I'm told.
I have big floppy ears,
And fluffy fur in layers.
I wag my tail to say hello,
And run to fetch the balls you throw.
I'm always looking for things to chew,
Your toy, a cushion, a shoe or two!
I'm as nosy as a cat,
But I'm your little puppy – and that's that!

A. Tick the correct answer for each question below.

1. Which sentence best summarises the poem?
   a. A little puppy introduces itself.
   b. A child describes a pet.
2. Which sentence is NOT needed to describe what Cuddles looks like?
   a. I have big floppy ears.
   b. I'm three months old.
   c. I wag my tail to say hello.
   d. I have fluffy fur in layers.
3. Which describing words best summarise what kind of puppy Cuddles is?
   a. lazy, nosy and old
   b. angry and unfriendly
   c. playful, friendly and young
   d. thin and fluffy

B. Write **T** for true and **F** for false.

1. Cuddles is a playful cat. ____
2. Cuddles is a playful puppy. ____
3. Puppies can sing very well. ____
4. Cuddles loves chewing things. ____

 ISBN 978-93-5103-600-5

12.4 Concluding

To understand a text better, you make conclusions, which are the decisions you make by working out the details given in the text. This is called concluding.

Read the narrative.

Grandfather Pat has a beautiful garden. He looks after the flower bed every day. He waters the plants and he pulls out weeds. He even talks to the plants!

One morning, Grandfather Pat noticed something strange. Some of the plants in his flower bed were lying flat. The next morning, the same thing happened to more plants. Who could have done it? Grandfather Pat decided to find out.

That night, Grandfather Pat kept a lookout in the garden. At midnight, he saw two bright eyes shining in the dark. He switched on his torch. A big black cat was curled up in the flower bed! Grandfather Pat had solved the mystery!

Take Note
A narrative
- is a story.
- tells the story in the order in which things happen.
- usually ends with a problem being solved.

1. Answer the questions below.

   a. How can you conclude that Grandfather Pat loved his garden?

   ____

   b. Why did Grandfather Pat keep a lookout in his garden?

   ____

   c. What do you think made the plants lie flat?

   ____

Think!
In order to conclude, you find facts and details in the text and decide what they mean.

2. Write a word of your own that means the same as each word taken from the narrative above.

   a. beautiful: ____________ b. strange: ____________

 ISBN 978-93-5103-600-5

3. Add (.), (?) or (!) to the sentences below.

a. He even talks to the plants

b. That night, Grandfather Pat kept a lookout in the garden

c. Who could have done it

Let's Practise

Read the narrative.

Vani visits her aunt and uncle's farm every year. Her aunt gives her a job to do each time. This time, Vani is in charge of getting eggs from the coop. Every morning, she collects the freshly laid eggs in her basket and brings them carefully to her aunt.

One morning, when Vani reaches for an egg, the hen pecks Vani on her arm with its beak. Vani rushes to her aunt and tells her about the hen. Her aunt explains that the hen must have laid an egg that will hatch into a chick. Mother hens do not let people take those eggs. They sit on their eggs to help them hatch.

So what is Vani's new job at the farm? Looking after the mother hen!

Tick the correct answer for each question below.

A. Why does Vani go to the coop every morning?

1. to get the eggs
2. to feed the hens

B. Why does the hen peck Vani's arm?

1. The hen is hungry.
2. The hen is protecting her egg.

C. Why do you think Vani gets a new job at the farm?

1. because Vani was bad at her old job
2. because Vani now has to look after the hen

 ISBN 978-93-5103-600-5

13 Composition

1. Look at the picture and write sentences to answer the questions below. The words in the box will help you.

park	flowers	jogging	waving	smiling	bloom	spring

a. What is this place?

____

b. What are the two girls doing?

____

c. What season is it? Why do you think so?

____

d. Write a paragraph about the picture. You may use the words in the box.

____

____

____

____

____

 ISBN 978-93-5103-600-5

2. Look at the pictures given. Then write each step in the correct order. The words in the box below will help you.

eyes and eyebrows	face in the mirror	ears, neck and hair
face outline	colour picture	nose and mouth

Example 1. Look at your face in the mirror.

2. ______________________________

3. ______________________________

4. ______________________________

5. ______________________________

6. ______________________________

 ISBN 978-93-5103-600-5

3. Ira is writing a letter to Disha to invite her to a Holi party. Fill in the blanks using words from the box below to complete the letter. The picture will help you.

dry colours and water balloons	soaked in lots of different colours	all the neighbours on our street
in the park in front of my house	food and sweets	to a Holi party

B-10, South Town
New Delhi

1 March 2016

Dear Disha,

I'm writing to invite you and your family ________________.

The party will be held ________________________________

on Friday. ________________________________ will be there

to celebrate Holi together this year. We shall have lots of

________________________________ to play with. There will be

yummy ______________________ too!

The party will begin at 10 a.m. Don't forget to come in old clothes.

They will be ____!

See you soon!

Your friend,
Ira

 ISBN 978-93-5103-600-5

4. Fill in the blanks using words from the box below to complete Mrs Sharma's conversation with Dad.

it's her favourite place	climb up	she cannot come down
I can see a black cat	she comes down at dinnertime	

On Sunday, our neighbour Mrs Sharma rang our bell.

"Daisy is stuck on my roof! ____________ ____________________________.

Can you please help me?" she asked.

"What is Daisy doing on the roof?" asked Dad.

"____________________________.

She likes to sit up there and think," said Mrs Sharma.

"Does she go on the roof often?" asked Dad.

"She goes up there every afternoon. ____________________________ ____________________________," said Mrs Sharma.

"I shall bring my ladder and ____________________________," said Dad.

Dad climbed up to the roof.

"Can you see Daisy?" asked Mrs Sharma.

"____________________________, but I cannot see Daisy," said Dad.

"But the cat **is** Daisy!" said Mrs Sharma.

 ISBN 978-93-5103-600-5

5. Write ten sentences about any one of the topics below. Draw or paste in a picture about your topic in the box.

a. My pet
b. My best friend
c. My favourite hobby
d. A trip to the zoo

 ISBN 978-93-5103-600-5

Review 4

1. Read the description.

Tigers, lions, cheetahs, leopards, pumas and jaguars all belong to the cat family. Tigers have an orange coat with black stripes. Their favourite food is deer. Like tigers, leopards and pumas also like eating deer. Leopards have yellow or brown coats with black spots, while pumas have a plain brown coat. Cheetahs look very similar to leopards, but they have longer legs. They like to hunt gazelles. Jaguars have orange coats with black spots and like to hunt water hogs. Lions have yellow or orange coats and they like to hunt zebras. The babies of all these animals are called cubs.

a. Complete the table below with information from the text.

Cat	Name of baby animal	Favourite food	Colour of coat
tiger		deer	orange and black
		zebras	
cheetah	cub		yellow or brown with black spots
leopard			yellow or brown with black spots
puma	cub		
		water hogs	orange and black

b. Answer the questions below.

i. Which three kinds of cats have the same favourite food?

____

ii. Write down one similarity among all six kinds of cats.

____

iii. Write down one difference between jaguars and tigers.

____

 ISBN 978-93-5103-600-5

c. Read the sentences below. Write **T** for true and **F** for false.

i. The cheetah and the lion have similar coats. ____

ii. The jaguar and the tiger have two common colours in their coats. ____

iii. The leopard and the puma have different coats. ____

2. Read the explanation and answer the questions below.

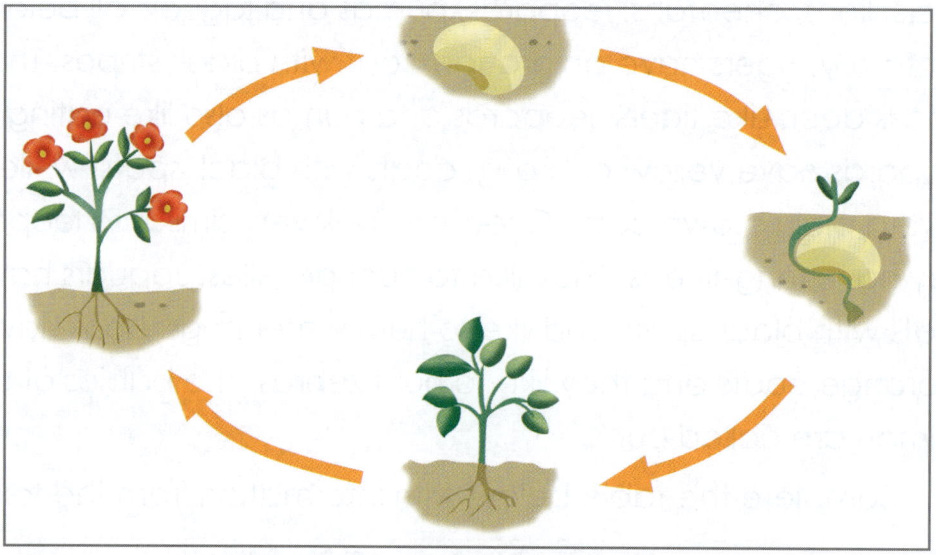

The Life Cycle of a Plant

1. A plant begins its life as a seed. Small changes happen inside the seed.

2. A tiny root grows downwards, and a tiny stem grows upwards. This small plant is called a seedling. It has a small stem with a few small leaves.

3. A seedling needs sunlight and water to grow. Slowly, the stem grows longer and new leaves appear. It becomes a full-grown plant.

4. Soon, flowers grow on the plant. Flowers help to make new seeds.

a. How does the life cycle of a plant begin?

____

b. What happens after small changes happen inside the seed?

____

c. What happens just before a seed becomes a full-grown plant?

____

d. How does the life cycle of a plant begin again?

____

 ISBN 978-93-5103-600-5

3. Read the narrative and answer the questions below.

Long ago, there was a prince who loved travelling to new places. One day, he set sail with his men in a wooden boat. After many days at sea, they spotted a beautiful island. Before they could reach the island, there was a storm. The boat tossed about on high waves. It was too heavy to sail in the storm. The prince asked his men to drop all their things into the sea. The prince dropped his golden crown too. Soon, the prince and his men were able to land safely on the island. They spotted a majestic animal among the trees. The prince named the animal Singa. He decided to make the island his home. He named it Singapura.

a. Which country do you think this narrative is about?

____

b. Why did the prince and his men drop things from the boat into the sea?

____

____

c. Tick the title that best summarises the narrative.

i. How Singapura got its name

ii. How a brave prince saved his life

d. Why did the prince name the island **Singapura**?

____

____

Spot the Error

e. There is a mistake in each sentence. Underline it and rewrite the sentence correctly in the blank below.

i. He set sail with his men in a woodden boat.

____

ii. The boat was too heavy to sail on the storm.

____

iii. The prince dropped its golden crown too.

____

iv. The prince named the island singapura.

____

 ISBN 978-93-5103-600-5

4. Write a letter to your friend inviting him or her to your birthday party.

____

____

____

Dear __________,

Your friend,

____

5. Look at the picture below. Write a paragraph about it.

 ISBN 978-93-5103-600-5

Word Power

Silent letters

Silent letters are letters that you can't hear when you say the word.

1. Unscramble the words with the help of the pictures given. Write them in the blanks and circle the silent letters.

a.  tubmh ________

b.  twrie ________

c. 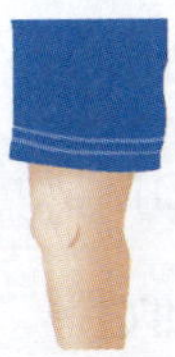 neke ________

d.  geridb ________

e. 8 tghie ________

f.  nkfie ________

g.  bmco ________

h.  csalte ________

i.  chtay ________

j.  falc ________

2. Make a sentence with each word below. Underline the silent letter in the word.

a. wrist: ________________________________

b. two: ________________________________

c. climb: ________________________________

d. whistle: ________________________________

e. walk: ________________________________

 ISBN 978-93-5103-600-5

Similar words

Similar words have almost the same meaning.

1. Circle the two similar words in each row below.

a.	build	jump	make	scare
b.	sleep	see	scream	look
c.	small	clean	funny	tiny
d.	leap	dive	jump	swim
e.	cook	drink	chew	munch
f.	sketch	paint	draw	peel
g.	big	old	huge	young
h.	glad	sad	sleepy	happy

2. Find similar words in the grid and write them in pairs in the blanks below.

pretty	shut	quiet	wealthy
quick	house	lovely	fat
tidy	fast	yell	hard
silent	neat	rich	plump
close	shout	home	difficult
sad	creep	right	long
tall	crawl	unhappy	correct

a. ____________________ h. ____________________

b. ____________________ i. ____________________

c. ____________________ j. ____________________

d. ____________________ k. ____________________

e. ____________________ l. ____________________

f. ____________________ m. ____________________

g. ____________________ n. ____________________

ISBN 978-93-5103-600-5

Opposites

Opposites are words with completely different meanings.

1. Write each word from the box next to its opposite in the table below.

south	none	subtract	old	answer	there	end
never	different	catch	far	late	low	false	narrow	dull

a.	add		i.	true	
b.	question		j.	wide	
c.	throw		k.	here	
d.	near		l.	same	
e.	early		m.	young	
f.	begin		n.	bright	
g.	always		o.	north	
h.	high		p.	all	

2. Tick the word that is the opposite in meaning to each word below.

a. short

i. small ii. tall iii. big

b. catch

i. drop ii. hold iii. get

c. closed

i. empty ii. end iii. open

d. buy

i. sell ii. give iii. gift

e. right

i. correct ii. false iii. wrong

f. lend

i. break ii. borrow iii. repair

 ISBN 978-93-5103-600-5

Same names

Some words have same names but different meanings.

Look at each pair of pictures given. Write down the same name in the blank below.

1.  ________ 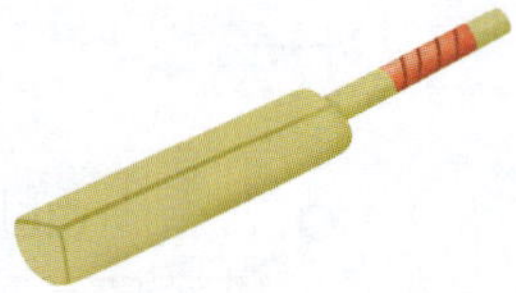

2.  ________ 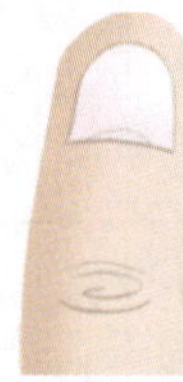

3.  ________ 

4.  ________ 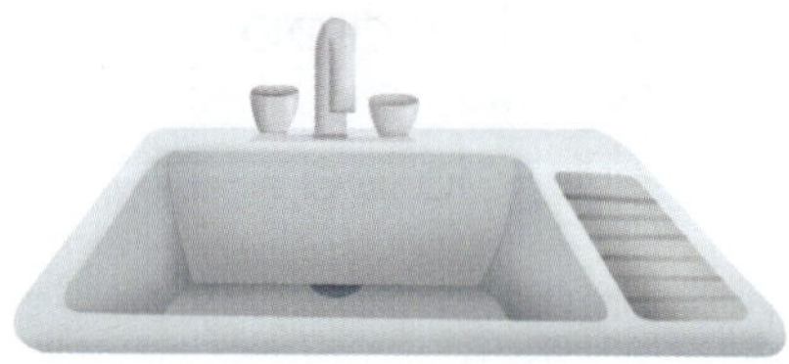

5. 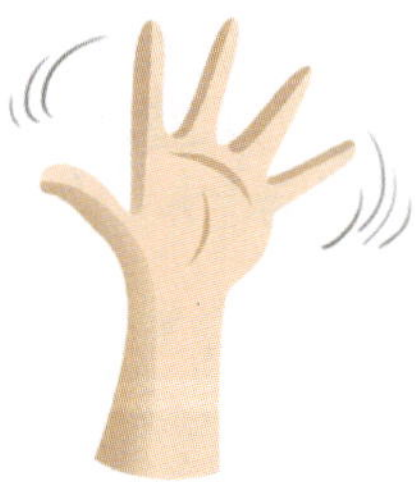 ________ 

 ISBN 978-93-5103-600-5